5 STEPS TO FINDING LOVE

A Holistic Guide for Women

Nicole Bayliss

5 Steps to Finding Love

First published in 2013 by Nicole Bayliss.

Published by Nicole Bayliss
c/o dosupport.com, PO Box 77, Cammeray, 2062, Australia

Email: info@wideawakesolutions.com.au
http://www.wideawakesolutions.com.au

Designed and edited by Daniel Olsson, dosupport.com
Cover design and graphics by Lina Hallberg,
Calina Design

Printed by Lightning Source

Bayliss, Nicole

ISBN 978-0-9875138-0-9

FOREWORD

This book expresses my sentiments and the purpose of my work as a kinesiologist and Emotional Intuitive Healer. Like Nicole, I have met and helped many women clear the emotional blocks, self-limiting belief systems and negative programming that prevents them being aligned to a successful, loving, committed relationship. It is only by going within, clearing the emotional and mental blocks and taking ownership of our issues, that we set ourselves free. As creators of our own reality, and by letting go, we act as agents of positive change within our lives. Nicole is able to identify the five powerful steps needed, with a number of life changing exercises to assist in quickly clearing self-sabotaging and mental/emotional blockages that may be preventing you from experiencing a fulfilling relationship on all levels. This book is ideal for all ages, men and women. If you are seeking that special someone in your life – this is the book to read!

Jacqui Prydie
Kinesiologist and Emotional Intuitive Healer

CONTENTS

Introduction ....

Step one 1

Step two 21

Step three..39

Step four 79

Step five 97

In conclusion.. 125

Action plan 127

Glossary of healing arts 133

About the author 135

INTRODUCTION

"I do not seek; I find." - *Pablo Picasso*

The inspirational artist, Pablo Picasso, knew something of immense importance. The more we search for something, the more it eludes us, or we may think we have found it, but it's not what we want. When we know exactly what it is we want, and we put our full trust in the Universe to provide us with what we need, and we follow through with aligned thoughts and behaviours, it never fails to answer.

Wanting to find a partner is a natural and normal desire, yet for many it is a wish that evades them. If you feel that it is never going to happen, you are not alone. I have met and counselled many women who feel disheartened or have even lost hope of ever finding the right person. Since starting a healing practice, the majority of my clients have been single women wanting to find a partner. At first I wondered why this particular demographic were being drawn to me. I have certainly had my own challenges around love, but I have also learned a lot and believe there are no accidents. I have brought the knowledge I have gained from my own personal experiences and healing journey into my professional work, and have found it to be not only helpful to my clients; it has aided them to heal themselves and successfully find love. So many women tell me they can't meet the right man, or feel constantly disappointed by relationships that don't work out. Why is it that in our modern world there are more ways than ever of meeting a man, yet it seems so difficult to find the right one? Why is it that we can be in a room full of eligible men or presented with a plethora of 'profiles' on a dating site, yet find no one who meets our criteria? So many are searching but not finding.

From my many healing sessions with single women, I began to ascertain some commonalities. Each of them had at least one of the following:

1. Issues around self-love – if we cannot love ourselves, then who will?

2. A belief that there were "no good men out there" and other negative beliefs - whatever we believe becomes our reality.

3. Unhealed wounds of the past that have sabotaged their choices – all lessons are repeated until learned.

4. A reluctance to take responsibility for the choices they have made in the past – until we take

responsibility for making poor choices, we will fail to make better ones.

5. An over-attachment to the desire for a mate – desperate energy is incapable of attracting the right person or the right relationship.

I aim to not only assist you in finding your ideal life partner, but also to help you find a greater level of life satisfaction and joy all round. As a Counsellor, NLP practitioner and Reiki Master, I believe that to maximise success, we must approach things holistically, from a range of aspects. In this book, I focus on:

- **Spiritual** – trusting in something higher that has our best interests at heart.

- **Psychological** – addressing unhealed wounds of the past which may be affecting the choices we are making in the present.

- **Energetic** – becoming aware of the energy we are giving out, and making changes within ourselves to ensure our energy is attracting to us what we want.

- **Behavioural** – choosing behaviours that will maximise success.

All aspects are interconnected. By trusting in something higher than ourselves, we feel supported in this lifetime, no matter what the outside circumstances may be. By clearing past issues, we choose different behaviour and our energy changes. When our energy changes, we attract new experiences. Throughout this book, I refer frequently to The Universe, but you can replace this word with God, Angels or whatever it is that you believe in. I will also be sharing with you some of my own personal story as well as those of my clients.

In each step, I have suggested exercises, some which involve writing. It's a good idea to buy a writing book that can become your journal of self-exploration. Excavating yourself through writing is healing in itself, and it can be gratifying to look back on a journal in weeks, months or years to come, and acknowledge just how far you have come.

"You need not leave your room. Remain at your table and listen. You need not even listen, simply wait, just learn to become quiet, still and solitary. The world will freely offer itself to you to be unmasked. It has no choice; it will roll in ecstasy at your feet." – Franz Kafka

To find love, you do not need to "do something" or "make things happen". Such actions are useless if your core beliefs and conscious thoughts are in conflict with what you are doing. The essence of the five steps is for you to attract what you want into your life through changing yourself on the inside. While Step Five is about our outside experience, it is a natural extension to the internal changes that must be made first. It is my hope that in reading this book and being willing to be totally honest with yourself, you will find the necessary pieces of the puzzle that have been evading you.

5 STEPS TO FINDING LOVE

1. **Have a love affair with yourself** – Learn to fill yourself up from the inside first.

2. **Change your beliefs** - Make change on the inside in order to change what's happening on the outside.

3. **Change your patterns** – Address the choices you have made in the past and begin to make better choices.

4. **Clarify what it is you want** – Become clear on your desires and set your goals.

5. **Make wise choices in the present** – Learn to be happy, present and true to yourself.

STEP ONE

HAVE A LOVE AFFAIR WITH YOURSELF

Learn to fill yourself up from the inside first

"You cannot be lonely, if you like the person you're
alone with."
- Dr Wayne Dyer

The most important of all qualities if we want to find
love is self-love. Whatever exists within us attracts its
likeness. Whatever is happening inside of you will
manifest outside of you. Self-love is the greatest attractor
of love there is. What is love? Love is a powerful force
that has the power to transform. To love ourselves we
must believe in love. It is only by loving ourselves that
we can extend that love to another. How should we love
ourselves? We can love ourselves by treating ourselves
the way we would like our beloved to treat us. Most of us
want kindness, affection, patience and understanding, but
how many of us give these things to ourselves? We are
often hard on ourselves, and engage in negative self-talk
and self-blame. Have you ever noticed the tone of your

1

inner voice? Is it kind, or is it harsh? Many women actually loathe themselves. Until we can learn to love ourselves, we cannot attract real love into our lives, because self-love comes from the very same source as the love we receive from outside of ourselves.

Some of us have been raised to believe that loving ourselves is a selfish act, and we must put loving others ahead of loving ourselves. In fact we must love and give to ourselves first before we love and give to others. I am not referring here to narcissism, which is an extreme form of selfishness. Self-love requires us to fill ourselves up from the inside so as to be whole people and capable of extending love to others. Narcissistic people are empty on the inside and prey on others to fill them up. When we don't fully love ourselves, we attract into our life people who are also not capable of fully loving us (or themselves), and we in turn are not capable of fully loving them. When we are harsh and criticising of ourselves, we are harsh and criticising of others.

Filling Ourselves Up from the Inside First

People who do not love themselves seek to fill the empty hole within them by having relationships out of need because they mistakenly think that someone else can make them whole, when in fact the only person who can do this is themselves. Being in a relationship with someone who doesn't love themselves is like trying to fill a bucket with a hole in it. They are overly needy, and constantly seek acceptance and validation from their partner, but it's never enough – the proverbial bucket is never filled – and the relationship becomes drained.

Throughout our lives, many of us have taken on messages that we are not lovable. Sabina came to see me after a failed relationship. She admitted to me that she could be possessive and controlling; behaviours that don't allow real love to flourish. Giving one's partner freedom is an act of love. Sabina's boyfriend ended their relationship, telling her he felt suffocated by her demands. When I asked Sabina how her relationship was with herself, she wasn't sure what I was talking about. She had always looked for validation outside of herself. She relied on her partner to tell her all the positive things she wanted to hear. "But how do you feel about yourself?" I asked. She contemplated the question for a while and then said that she probably didn't like herself very much. Sabina revealed that she was raised in a family where her parents were emotionally distant and she was rarely praised and often criticised. As a child we take on messages directly and wholly. "If there was a message you got from your parents, what was it?" I asked. She replied through tears "You are not worth being around or being listened to". Looking back on her past family experiences, Sabina could see that she was a normal, loving child and that her parents had not given her the love that she deserved.

All children want to be noticed and know that they matter, but many don't receive this vital message from their parents. Sabina had been carrying this incorrect belief all her life, and as a result had attracted and created similar relationships. Sabina attracted emotionally distant men and became needy and clingy in relationships, hoping her partner would fill the empty hole within her, while also fearing he would leave her. Her behaviour became a self-fulfilling prophecy. In our sessions together, Sabina set about healing herself and filling herself up with love from the inside first. She replaced her old childhood belief of "I am not worth being around or being listened to" to "I am worthy of love".

Acknowledging the Shadow

Anyone can learn to love themselves, no matter what incorrect messages they have taken on during childhood or later on. Most of us have aspects of ourselves that we are in denial about. The transpersonal psychologist Carl Jung named this unknown part of ourselves "the shadow". Many of us are in denial of our shadow, or at least some aspects of it, because it can be a painful experience to confront it. The shadow contains the parts of ourselves we have hidden away for a very long time – we got the message very early that these parts of ourselves would make us "unlovable". However, if we don't confront it, it will control us on a subconscious level, and sabotage our lives. We need to learn to love and accept every part of ourselves. It is only by doing this that we can love and accept every part of our future partner. The more we can love about ourselves, the greater our potential to love another. We must acknowledge that we are human, and while we may like the parts of ourselves that are kind, giving, creative, knowledgeable, helpful and positive, it's also important to acknowledge the shadow parts such as anger, selfishness, laziness, ignorance and negativity. We ALL have within us the yin and the yang. By acknowledging all parts of yourself, not only will the negative traits stop controlling you on a subconscious level; you will be able to control them and even use these traits effectively. Sometimes we NEED to get angry, or be lazy or selfish. By acknowledging the yin and the yang within you, you become a whole person, accepting all parts of yourself and willing to accept all parts of others. That is not to say that you should put up with ill treatment; simply that you become more understanding and accepting of others and their "humanness".

I have been single for two significant periods of my life. Up until my late twenties when I got married, and during my mid-forties after a divorce. It was during this second single period that I finally came to terms with my shadow. During my marriage, I endeavoured to be the perfect wife and mother, denying the other parts of myself that I felt were unlovable. Forever "doing" for others and rarely giving to myself, I swallowed my resentment most of the time until I got caught by surprise by my own out-of-control shadow. I fell passionately in love and left my marriage, causing chaos and pain for my now ex-husband and my three children.

Had I acknowledged my shadow earlier – my need for fun, passion, self-expression, freedom and love, my marriage may have worked or it may have ended even sooner, but it wouldn't have ended in the disastrous and sudden way it did. However, it was during my mid-life crisis that I sought to heal myself, and subsequently find my purpose in healing. Since embracing my shadow, I no longer feel the need to please others, I make no apologies for who I am and I now attract into my life loving, accepting people.

If you feel that you were given messages in the past that you weren't lovable or worthy, the following exercise is designed to help you heal those incorrect messages that you were given.

❧

Exercise 1

Letting Go of Old Incorrect Messages about Self Love

Close your eyes and imagine the timeline of your life, starting with your birth and leading all the way to now, and then carrying on into the future. Step onto your timeline to the point that is NOW. Allow yourself to float up above your timeline and look back to your past. Float along your timeline to your

earliest memory of feeling unloved and getting the message that you weren't lovable. Perhaps you were a young child, and have a particular memory or image of this. I want you to find your earliest and most powerful memory of getting a message that you were not lovable. Float above the event and watch the event happening with you in it. Notice what each person in the situation is doing. Allow yourself to take in the perspectives of everyone involved in the event. Allow your subconscious mind to take in any learnings. Now drop down into the event. Is there anything you would like to say to your younger self? Perhaps you can tell this younger self that they are receiving an incorrect message and that they are lovable. Do they need a hug? Give to your younger self what it is you would have wanted back then. Now rise above your timeline and float along towards the NOW and on the way, notice that all the times when you have felt unlovable or unloved are being healed as you float along to the NOW. Now look towards your future, and know that from now on, your life will be lived in the knowledge that you are loved and lovable.

❦

Self Esteem

Self-love means having a healthy self-esteem. Self-esteem is the inner knowledge that you are worthy and that you matter in this world. People with good self-esteem value themselves enough to leave a job that they are miserable in, or be on their own rather than compromise their values to be in a relationship that is not in their highest good. Self-esteem is something that some of us have had a head start on, and some of us a handicap. Most of us have at least a few issues around our self-worth and may need to work on it at certain points in our lives. Our self-esteem raises every time we make a choice that is in our highest good, each time we choose to improve or better ourselves, each day we live in alignment with our values and work towards our goals.

Loving and Accepting Our Physical Self

Do you like the way you look? Unless we learn to love and accept our physical appearance and our body, and to respect it by eating well, exercising and looking after it, how can we expect someone else to love and accept it? Some parts of our bodies we may not be able to change. It is time to stop comparing yourself to others, to look in the mirror and thank the Universe for what you have. When we choose to compare ourselves, we are unlikely to be happy with the way we are. There is always going to be someone more beautiful, slim, intelligent or youthful. Magazines displaying beautiful women with perfect bodies don't help the cause because they are only depicting a certain look. There are many other looks, and they are beautiful too.

❧

Exercise 2

The Mirror Exercise

Stand in front of a mirror first thing in the morning. Come close to the mirror and look at your face. Say:

"(your name), I love you."

If you feel you can't say it, start with:

"(your name), I like you."

If that doesn't feel right for you, begin with:

"(your name), each day I am learning to like you more and more."

It's important to start with what feels real for you and to leave scope for future possibilities.

Do this exercise every day.

Now look at your body. Notice everything you like about your body. Thank the Universe for giving you the parts of yourself that you like.

If you have any aspects of your physical self that you don't like, take some time to look at these parts. Acknowledge that Perfection on a human level exists only by the standards of beauty that are dictated in this particular age, but in the spiritual and energetic realm, we are all perfect. Acknowledge that you are perfect and made exactly as you were meant to be for this lifetime.

∽

Do you love yourself enough to look after yourself, by maximising your physical beauty with clothes you love, makeup that enhances your face and a hairstyle that suits you? Some may say that "looks shouldn't matter", but the way you look is the visual aspect of you. While true beauty lies deeper in a person, most of us are attracted initially by what we see, so making the most of ourselves on the outside is still important. Cosmetic surgery has become a common practice. If choosing the surgical route to enhance physical appearance, it is important to excavate what the intention is. So many women are having cosmetic surgery in a quest for physical perfection. Because physical perfection doesn't exist, surgical procedures can become an addiction. Women addicted to cosmetic surgery tend to attract not only men who rate a woman on her physical appearance alone, but men who prey on insecurity. When I see a face or body that has been overly enhanced by cosmetic surgery, I see a lack of self-acceptance and love. I am not referring here to everyone who has undergone cosmetic procedures.. Surgery for something that has contributed to a person's low self-esteem for a long time can be helpful and empowering. Ruth, 67, decided to have a facelift because she felt her sagging skin hid the energetic and beautiful person who still existed on the inside. Vivienne had surgery on a large nose that she felt had overpowered her face for years and Sharon had breast augmentation because she didn't like her flat chest. All three women were very happy with the results and felt the decision enhanced their lives. Real beauty emanates from a person who has a healthy glow and a positive attitude. How many times have you met someone who you didn't find that physically attractive to begin with, but as you got to know them they became more attractive?

Never have we been so obsessed about body weight than we are now. Never has the human race experienced such an obesity epidemic. When I see an overweight person, I see a person whose life is out of balance. When somebody is addicted to food, they are endeavouring to fill themselves up; unfortunately it's with the wrong substance. Their emptiness has nothing to do with their stomach; it has to do with disconnectedness and deep wounds of the past. This is why diets rarely work in the long term. We are only dealing with the issue on a superficial level, not at the core level. When someone tells me that they're going to lose weight, I ask them what they usually do when they lose something. The answer is, of course, they try and find it. I ask them to re-word their intention to become "slim" or "light". Many people struggle with weight issues all their lives, but this is not a reason not to love themselves. Loving yourself means loving yourself exactly as you are right here and now. Be kind to yourself about why you are the way you are. If you think you're going to start loving yourself "when I lose weight", it's never going to happen. It has to be the other way around. Love yourself first. This happened to my client, Samantha who, once she began her healing journey with talking therapy and Reiki, began to make better lifestyle choices and became the size she wanted to be.

Learn to Appreciate and Enjoy Your Life Exactly as it is Right Now

Julie came to see me for Reiki. She was 33 and single and most of her friends were married and having children. When she socialised with them, she felt like the odd one out. They would talk about "baby stuff". More and more she felt she had less in common with them, although she wanted what they had. "Being around them reminds me of everything I don't have," she told me. She decided to spend less time with her married girlfriends, and more time at home in front of the TV. "Some weekends I don't do anything." Julie was lonely. She was moving on from her old friends, but hadn't replaced them with anything or anyone. The more lonely and depressed she felt, the more passive she became about creating a new life for herself. She was focusing on what she didn't have, instead of focusing on what she did have. I asked Julie to consider that just because her friends were married and having babies, it didn't mean that their lives were idyllic. Every stage of life has its share of challenges. Julie was viewing her friends' lives as "good" and hers as "bad". I told her that shortly after I finally achieved my "dream" of getting married and having my first child, it was anything but the "high" I thought it would be. I felt isolated, lonely, exhausted and depressed. I sought the company of other young mothers because only they seemed to be able to relate to the personal difficulties I was going through. What Julie saw as a cliquey, exclusive group that she couldn't relate to, I could see as a group of women supporting each other through a significant and difficult life change. Their situation wasn't any "better" than Julie's; just different. It was important for Julie to begin to appreciate what life could offer her as a single woman in her 30's, even if her desire was to find her life partner and have children.

If you aren't happy with what you have right now, it's unlikely you'll be happy when you achieve your goals. So many of us live with the belief that "I will be happy when...", only to find that we're not happy when we achieve what we thought would make us happy. Happiness is fleeting – it comes and goes, no matter what happens; even after we have achieved our goals. Fulfilment and inner peace are more realistic and worthier goals. In fact, when I talk about happiness that is what I am referring to. It's important to learn to love and appreciate exactly where you're at in life. Being single doesn't mean you have to be "unhappy", unfulfilled or without peace. In fact, there are many fabulous things about being single.

- A time to explore your interests and passions.

- A time to get to know yourself.

- A time to focus on your career and life purpose.

- A time to focus on meaningful friendships and expanding your social circle.

- A time to enjoy the freedom to do what you want whenever you want.

A period of being single between relationships is healthy. It gives you time to get to know yourself again, to reflect on lessons learned, heal from past hurts and create a life for yourself that you love. Feeling fulfilled while you are single is also going to help you find a mate. For me, it wasn't until I began to fall in love with my own life that I began to attract in potential partners.

Loneliness

Feelings of loneliness are likely to come up, particularly at times when you are grieving a relationship that hasn't worked out, there are no friends or family around to see, or you're not used to being on your own. The feeling of loneliness can arise from negative self-talk such as "I'm a loser because I'm home alone on a Saturday night" or "I'm not lovable because no one's called me in three days". When this happens, notice any negative self-talk and replace it with kind words. At some point in our lives, we all must face our "aloneness". When we feel lonely, it can seem that we are the only person in the world who is experiencing this, and that everybody else seems to be out there having a great time. But the truth is that everyone, at some point in their lives, goes through feelings of loneliness. People who are fearful of being alone will seek out others' company, keep themselves busy or resort to addictions - anything to avoid facing the feeling of loneliness. While it's good to connect with others, we need to be mindful of our intention. Is it because we really want to see others, or is it because we're fearful of being alone? Some people, if they cannot be alone with themselves, end up living their lives out of fear, avoiding truly knowing themselves and robbing themselves of an authentic life. Often their avoidance strategy begins to fail them and they find themselves facing a personal crisis far greater than if they faced their own aloneness to begin with. There is nothing wrong with being alone or feeling lonely. If you want to be a whole person, you will have to feel the full range of emotions, including that of loneliness.

The relationship I left my marriage for didn't last and I found myself single, alone and experiencing grief at age 47, something I had never envisaged. My children would spend every alternate week at their father's house and I would book up my social plans in advance in order to have company almost every night, for fear of being alone and facing myself and my grief. I dreaded people cancelling plans on me, which would inevitably happen. I would sit on my own in front of the television until I went to bed. Slowly I became aware that it didn't have to be like this. Instead of thinking "How do I get through this evening?" I could ask myself "How can I make this evening really great?" I felt excited and would plan a wonderful evening just for me. I would shop in my local markets for my favourite food in the afternoon, have a long soak in a bubble bath surrounded by scented candles, cook myself a delicious meal while listening to music I loved, watch a DVD that wasn't chosen by my kids, and fall into bed with a good book. I would wake up early and go down to my local beach to swim before I went to work. I began to feel truly blessed and appreciative of this time in my life.

Being OK with loneliness is a big bonus when you do enter into a relationship, because there are times in relationships where we also feel lonely. The ability to 'self-soothe' when we feel alone is a wonderful tool to have. In fact, studies have shown that this ability to self-soothe is a major factor in the longevity of long-term relationships.

∾

Exercise 3

Dealing with Loneliness

If the feeling of loneliness remains, sit with it and feel the feeling in your body. It is natural to want to run from the feeling and yet the best thing you can do is to sit with it and feel it. Relax your shoulders and imagine your heart opening up to fully experience the feeling. Notice it is only a feeling, and feelings pass. By feeling it deeply, you allow the feeling to pass through you and to clear. Allow the feeling to just be there, knowing that it will pass. If you disallow the feeling, it remains trapped in your body as an energetic block that can be triggered on a regular basis.

∾

Sorrow and Grief

At some point we all experience feelings of sadness, whether it be from a disappointment in love, the end of a relationship or feelings of hopelessness. When sadness comes, honour it by accepting it and feeling it. We cannot know love without knowing pain. Rumi expresses this perfectly in his poem:

The way of love is not a subtle argument
The door there is devastation
Birds make great sky circles of their freedom
How do they learn it?
They fall, and falling, they're given wings.

Understand that sorrow clears away the past and our old beliefs that no longer serve us, making room for future joy.

Addictions

Addictions are a sign that we are struggling with self-love. It doesn't matter what the addiction is; we use it to mask emotional pain. Our addictions stop us from feeling. While drugs and alcohol are obvious addictions, others may not be so obvious. Workaholics mask their deep feelings of worthlessness by constantly being busy and achieving, love addicts use the "high" of infatuation to stop themselves from facing their issues and their pain, internet addicts go off into another world for hours at a time rather than face their reality, smokers use the experience of smoking to take their attention away from their emotions and gamblers hide from life by focusing their attention on their next bet. Dealing with an addiction is both confronting and painful. While drugs, alcohol and gambling can cause direct chaos in a person's life in a relatively short period of time, the "softer" addictions are more socially acceptable and not necessarily labelled as an addiction. We can be in denial of these for years before we start to see the full impact of them on our lives. What are your addictions and are you willing to explore the issues behind them?

During my divorce I became addicted to smoking. When I was in emotional pain, the first thing I did was reach for a cigarette. As I breathed in the smoke, I connected the experience with a feeling of being removed. Of course it didn't last long, and I would reach for the next cigarette. I call this "false healing". Our minds convince us that it will be good for us and that we need it because it makes us feel better. As long as we have the addiction, we aren't looking for more constructive ways to help ourselves deal with the intense feelings that are a part of life, and therefore avoid the underlying issues. It took me a few years to break this addiction, and the way it was broken was an interesting thing. I wrote, "stop smoking" in a list of five goals, put the list away and went about living life to its fullest, focusing on my family, my new relationship, my wellbeing and my work. Six months later, I was a non-smoker. This had happened organically and naturally. Giving up was such a non-event that I didn't actually notice I was a non-smoker for at least six weeks! The more we heal ourselves, the more we will love and accept ourselves, and the better our life choices will be.

Further Suggestions for Self Love

- Write down every positive quality you have. Read the list each day and add to the list as new ones come to light.

- Be your own best friend. Praise yourself whenever you have finished a task or achieved a goal. This reminds you that you are moving forward and growing. Compliment yourself when you look good, smile at yourself in the mirror and be kind to yourself when you are feeling low. Do all the things a good friend would do.

- Look into activities, hobbies or clubs that interest you and do at least one. This will expand your world, open up opportunities for new friendships and enrich you as a person. You could even meet your potential partner through this, and if so, you have met someone who shares your passion!

- Learn to enjoy your own company. Cook yourself your favourite meal, light candles, burn incense, take a bubble bath, play your favourite music. Create a beautiful atmosphere just for you.

- Rose essential oil works on the same vibration as love. It can be burned in an oil burner or diluted and applied to the skin.

STEP TWO

CHANGE YOUR BELIEFS

Make change on the inside in order to change what's happening on the outside

"People do not see the world as it is, they see it as they are."
- Anais Nin

How many times have you said or heard the following statements?

- "There's just no good men out there."

- "All the good ones are taken."

- "All men are bastards."

- "The ones I like don't like me."

- "I'm never going to meet anybody worthwhile."

Whatever you believe, the universe will match it. Before long, your "belief" *is* your reality. What the universe sends you just keeps reinforcing what you believe and it becomes a vicious cycle. I was invited to a friend's home for Christmas drinks and sat on the sofa with two ladies who were a similar age to me. I had recently become single, and after half an hour with these two, I felt drained and depressed. "There aren't any good men around," said one. "I know," said the other. "When you get to our age, there's just no one available." They went on to tell me about every dating disaster they had experienced over the past few years. I cannot recall one positive statement during our conversation and their world-weary faces reflected their beliefs. When I tried to intervene with a positive remark, I was shot down with "That's what you think, but just you wait until you've been single as long as we have." My hostess looked aggrieved when I said I had to go. I walked out of her house feeling heavy and low. Driving home, I realised that I had been taking on their negative energy and my desire to get out of there was my own spirit protecting me. Negative energy can be catchy. It's important to beware of the company you keep and the messages you are taking on!

What are your beliefs about relationships? Do any of them sound like this?

- "Relationships are hard work."

- "I'm not good at relationships."

- "Men like to date me, but don't want to commit to me."

- "Everyone else seems to be in a relationship except me."

- "Always the bridesmaid, never the bride."

- "I'm frightened of making another mistake."

You might reply "Yes, but it's true." Of course it's true – for you. That's what you believe and that's what you're getting in return from the Universe. Perhaps you didn't once believe these things, but through some negative relationship experiences, you acquired a belief around that. This is what's happening:

1. You have a negative relationship experience.
   (Let's say a relationship with a man who doesn't treat you well).

2. You take on a belief about that negative relationship experience.
   ("I don't want another man to treat me badly in a relationship").

3. The Universe gives you another negative relationship experience in answer to your belief.
   (It doesn't hear the word "don't"; it hears "man to treat me badly in a relationship").
   (Along comes another man who doesn't treat you well).

4. Your belief is reinforced.
   ("The only men I get are the ones who treat me badly").

5. The Universe gives you another negative relationship experience and so on.

What we fear, we attract to us. When we feel high emotion about something, be it fear, excitement or love, we put it out to the universe with an extra charge and the universe delivers with an extra charge, so if you are holding any fears about relationships, the universe will deliver to you what it is you fear. The Universe also sends us anything that we particularly DO NOT want. When we say we DON'T want something, the Universe doesn't hear the "don't" nor any other negative. It just hears the SOMETHING. On an energetic level, if we are feeling negative or fearful, we are carrying around with us a cloud of dark, murky energy that attracts other clouds of dark, murky energy. We must clear our own energy in order to attract in clear, loving energy.

Not all of our beliefs are caused by negative relationship experiences. Many of them come from our childhood experiences or our inherited beliefs from our parents. Some of these beliefs are buried deep in our subconscious. To change negative beliefs, we don't necessarily need to know where they came from or why, but we do need to become aware of them in order to change them. Once we become aware of our negative beliefs, we have the power to change them, and this can powerfully alter the course of our lives.

Gemma came to see me after a string of relationships in which she was betrayed. Gemma felt understandably frightened of being hurt again. "Men always cheat on me" was one of Gemma's beliefs and she wanted to turn this belief around. "All men are trustworthy" was not a realistic replacement. On a rational level, Gemma knew that trustworthy men existed as her sister and best friend had married men she considered trustworthy. Gemma also acknowledged that through her belief, she was attracting only untrustworthy men into her life. Through this awareness, she created an affirmation: "I now only attract trustworthy men into my life".

Believing We Deserve

When I met Penny, 40, she had been suffering from depression and taking antidepressants for two years. She told me that she had only ever had a few brief relationships, and felt like a failure. Talking about her childhood, she said she had a twin sister who was shy and not as intelligent or as pretty as Penny. Throughout her childhood, whenever Penny wanted to do anything, her mother would insist that her twin sister go along also. Penny found this to be a drain and wanted to be her own person, but at the same time felt guilty for being selfish. To make matters worse, whenever she achieved anything, she was never praised, as her parents didn't want to upset her twin sister who didn't do as well.

Penny felt guilty whenever she did well at anything. Needless to say, she struggled in her career as well as relationships, and was constantly overlooked for promotion. I suggested to her that many years ago as a child she formed the opinion that she wasn't worthy of love, praise or achievement. Penny could see that at a very deep level, she had been carrying this belief around with her all her life, and she'd been sabotaging her desires for years. Whenever she did meet someone she liked, on a subconscious level she felt she didn't deserve them and it would be over shortly after it began. Whenever we hold such hidden beliefs, our conscious goals are rarely realised because at a deeper level, that belief is running the show. By bringing unconscious beliefs to conscious awareness, we are almost at the cure. Wanting to make up for lost time, Penny created an affirmation for herself. "I deserve passionate, adoring, wonderful love." Penny is now off anti-depressants, has been promoted at work and has been in a relationship for eight months. When we heal something at core level, everything begins to change for the better.

Making it Impossible

Julia had the opposite problem to Penny. She met and went out with plenty of men, and proceeded to give me a long list of each of their faults. Max had a great career but wasn't good looking enough, Tom had been good looking but not ambitious enough, Jeremy was good looking and ambitious but didn't talk enough, Harry was perfect in every way but she didn't feel enough of a connection. The more I listened, I picked up that Julia was looking for the "perfect man" who didn't exist, and she was making it impossible for herself to have a relationship. "Do you think you may have an underlying belief that no one will ever be good enough?" I asked. "No," she said, "he just hasn't come along yet." My instinct told me that Julia was commitment phobic, and she used the "not good enough" tag to avoid going deeper into a relationship with anyone. I told Julia what my thoughts were. She didn't come back again.

"The One" and Soul Mates

Vicky, 33, hadn't had a relationship in eight years. She told me that she had met "the one" ten years ago, but it hadn't worked out. His name was Richard and she had never felt such deep love for anyone since. I asked Vicky what she meant by "the one". "You know," she replied, "my soul mate, the person I was meant to spend the rest of my life with". I suggested to Vicky that if she was meant to spend the rest of her life with Richard, she would be. Clearly it didn't work out, and she was meant to move on. Why hadn't she? Vicky had limited her potential to find love for years because of a belief that we are meant to meet and fall in love with one person in this lifetime, and this past boyfriend was "the one". Therefore she had missed her chance at love. Such an overly romantic view of life doesn't serve us. In fact, it limits our options and even if we do end up being with the person we perceive to be "the one", it puts unrealistic expectations on that person. Whoever we choose to be with, no matter how well suited, sooner or later the relationship will face some challenges. Vicky asked me if I believed in soul mates and I replied that on a spiritual level, I did believe in them. However, we can have many soul mates in one lifetime in many forms - platonic friends, colleagues or lovers. Soul mates come into our lives to teach us something – be it a lesson in love or a lesson in life. I asked her if she could view Richard as a soul mate who came to teach her about love, and that perhaps there were other soul mates in the world waiting to meet her. Vicky cried as she reluctantly let go of her old belief about Richard, but eventually she felt lighter and freer.

❧

Exercise 4

Excavating and Changing your Beliefs about Men and Relationships

Write on a page in a notebook: What are my beliefs about relationships?

Be honest and write down everything you can think of, both positive and negative.

On the next page, write: What are my beliefs about men?

When you have finished writing these lists, sit quietly and examine them. Notice any beliefs that are not serving you. Ask yourself "Where did this come from?" Even if you can't answer that question, you have created awareness around this belief, and from awareness, you have the power to do something about it.

In your journal, create a new belief to replace the old, self-limiting belief. Let these new beliefs become affirmations. Read them back and say them to yourself each day for a week. Whenever you feel the old beliefs creeping in, pick up your notebook and re-read your positive affirmations.

Here are some examples of positive affirmations:

- My perfect partner is coming into my life in divine and perfect timing.

- Loving relationships are easy for me.

- My loving and positive energy attracts a loving and positive partner in return.

- I allow my ideal partner into my life.

- From now on, I attract only kind, loving, faithful and generous men into my life.

- I let go of all past relationship traumas and welcome the blessings of new loving relationships into my life.

∽

Why Do You Want a Relationship?

Have you ever asked yourself why you want a relationship? What are your *beliefs* about what a relationship will do for you? Do any of these feel true for you?

- I will be happy when I am in a relationship.

- When I find a relationship, I won't feel lonely anymore.

- It will make my family happy when/if I get married.

- All my friends are getting married and I want to be married too.

- A new relationship will help me get over my past relationship.

If any of these beliefs feel like your truth, you may find yourself disappointed when you do enter into a relationship. Unless you can learn to be happy on your own, a relationship won't make you any happier in the long run. If we're empty on the inside as a single person, we're still going to be empty on the inside when we're in a relationship. While being in a relationship will be different to being single, it won't necessarily be better. Relationships don't fix things. Whatever is not working for you now will be brought into a relationship and need to be healed at some point. Wanting a relationship to fill the void of loneliness will not fill it for long. Loneliness is a feeling that can also occur in a relationship. It is better to deal with your loneliness as a single person rather than enter a relationship to alleviate it. Be sure that you want a long-term partner for the right reasons, and your reasons only. There is no need to follow the crowd. We may be unaware that we're dancing to the beat of someone else's drum unless we take the time to go within and ask the question "Why do I want a relationship?" This will uncover our true intentions.

When I asked this question to my client Mandi, she replied "Because I'm 32 and I should have a partner and family." Whenever I hear someone use the word "should", they are revealing that they are making choices based on someone else's values. "Why *should* you, Mandi?" I asked'. After some deep exploration, she discovered that she didn't actually want a partnership all that much. She loved the single life and her freedom. In our society, we are constantly bombarded with the idea that we aren't complete unless we partner up with someone. Friends and family can even look at us with pity when we are single. "I thought I was unhappy because I was single," said Mandi, "but I'm beginning to realise that I'm unhappy because of all the pressure and expectation from my family." Mandi instantly felt better, because she realised she didn't have to live her life based on other peoples' expectations. "If I meet and fall in love with someone, that would be lovely, but I'd also be happy to remain single." Choices made based on other people's truths or expectations are always the wrong ones. While people share similarities, we are also different. We are here to experience and learn different things and to enjoy the journey of life in our own unique way. Always be true to yourself, and yourself only, when choosing what you want. Here are some positive reasons for wanting a relationship:

- I want to share my life with someone.

- I want a family.

- I want to know someone intimately, and for them to know me intimately.

- I want romance, love and companionship.

- I've had a wonderful time as a single person, and now I want to experience a partnership.

- I'm ready to settle down.

- I want to love and be loved.

∾

Exercise 5

Why do I want a Relationship?

In your notebook, write down all the reasons why you want a relationship. Read through your list. If any of your answers reveal a belief that a relationship will "fix" you or your life, cross it out and write a new belief, acknowledging what you need to heal and also acknowledging your desire for a relationship if that is what you want.

For example, "I want a relationship because I feel lonely" could be replaced with "I acknowledge my loneliness, which I am in the process of healing. I look forward to a healthy, loving relationship."

⌘

Reframing Your Thoughts

Changing your beliefs so as to bring you into alignment with your authentic self will make you a happier person. It's also important to become aware of your day-to-day thoughts, as you are constantly attracting into your life that which you think about. This doesn't mean we must replace negative thoughts with unrealistic positive thinking; rather, we need to look at the world through a different lens. Fear and low expectations will deliver to us what we don't want. They are also not the truth. The Universe only wants what is best for us and is eager to give us what we want. Negative thoughts interrupt the flow of the Universe and prevent us from receiving what it is we want.

Whenever you find yourself feeling negative about not having met your partner yet, it is a sign that you are not in the positive energetic flow of the Universe. Have you noticed that as soon as you've experienced a negative thought, it changes how you feel in your body? In fact, it changes the chemistry of your body! In order to receive what the Universe is offering, you MUST BE in the positive Universal flow by feeling as good as you can. You can do this by reframing your thoughts.

Here are some examples of a negative thought and their positive reframe:

1. "Another relationship ended. Now I'm back on the shelf and going to have to go through the same thing all over again."
   Could be turned around to:
   "That was a lucky escape and a lesson learned. Now I'm free to find a person who's right for me."

2. "I'm never going to meet anyone who really cares."
   Could be turned around to:
   "From my experiences with uncaring men in relationships, I'm now clear that the most important quality a potential partner needs to have is a caring attitude."

3. "I can't believe I went out with such an idiot. What was I thinking?"
   Could be turned around to:
   "I can't believe how much I've grown. Two years ago I thought he was God's Gift and now I think he's a jerk. I've learned a lot."

4. "There must be something wrong with me. Relationships never work out."
   Could be turned around to:
   "I've attracted the wrong ones so far, but I'm healing myself and changing my beliefs and patterns."

If you are experiencing a negative thought (the key to this is how you're feeling in your body), stop! Backtrack to the thought. Reframe the thought to a more truthful, positive statement. Notice the feeling of relief in your body. Has this ever happened to you? A friend calls and tells you that she and her boyfriend have just got engaged. You hear yourself offer congratulations, but inside you're churned up and jealous, and thinking, "When is it going to be my turn?" You don't feel good by thinking the way you do, and that's because it's incorrect thinking. On an energetic level, like attracts like. Things that are happening around you are more likely to happen *to* you. So change your internal response to one of happiness and genuine goodwill and say to yourself "This is wonderful! It's getting closer to my turn."

Patience

When I met Sarah, she told me she was tired and fed up with waiting for a man to come into her life. She felt she had done everything possible to attract him in, including buying a king size bed, investing in the finest cotton sheets and making room in her walk-in wardrobe for "his clothes". I see many women who are "tired of waiting" to meet their partner. When we feel that we are "waiting" for something, that is exactly what the Universe gives us in return – waiting. Do not wait for anything or anyone. Live your life to the fullest every day and fill it with all the people, activities and things you love. That is how you "allow" someone into your life.

"Waiting" implies there is an empty space to be filled and that you are not already complete. By all means, clean out your cupboards and make your home as clean, streamline and comfortable as possible, but I disagree with clearing an empty space solely for the purpose of expecting someone, because it can create the opposite effect of what you want. Each day, it reminds you that he's not here yet. Timing doesn't always happen in the way we want it. Believe in Divine Universal Timing – the time that the Universe deems to be the right time. That way you can relax, knowing it is coming to you. It comes as no surprise when a client tells me that she met her partner "when I least expected it". It's usually at a time when your life is so full with other things going on that you have no time to wait or want too much.

STEP THREE

CHANGE YOUR PATTERNS

**Address the choices you have made in the past
and begin to make better choices**

"There are no mistakes, only lessons."
- Cherie Carter-Scott

In order to make better choices going forward, we must be willing to examine the choices we have made in the past and identify any that haven't served us. When you acknowledge that every choice you have made in your life has brought you to where you are now, you are taking responsibility for your current situation. When we don't take responsibility and blame our misfortunes on other people and circumstances, our lives are unlikely to improve as we are looking at life through a victim mentality, and it renders us powerless. That is not to say that bad things that are out of our control don't happen. They do, but it is what we do about them and what we learn from them that matter.

Look back on your past. Do you have a pattern of being attracted to a certain type? Each man you've been with may appear different on the outside, but when you get closer to him you realise he has similarities to previous partners. This is good news if you've had healthy, positive relationships, but a problem if your relationships have been unfulfilling ones. Very often we make unconscious choices based on unhealed wounds from our relationships with our father or mother. If your relationship with either of your parents has been a troubled one, it's likely that your romantic relationships will be troubled as well, unless you have addressed the inner wounds you are carrying. These wounds, when left unhealed, attract further wounds and the resulting build-up is what is known as "baggage". Baggage is not our past; it is our negative view and feelings about our past which we haven't let go. Carrying baggage ensures that all potential relationships are doomed to repeat the same old patterns.

Rachel came to see me for counselling. She was in a toxic relationship and she described her boyfriend James as selfish, arrogant and controlling. He liked everything his way and would dictate when they would see each other, where they went and what they would do. He didn't want to socialise with her friends and eventually she began seeing less and less of them. If she went out with her girlfriends he would call her to see where she was and what time she would be home. While demanded the very best of everything, including the food

Rachel prepared and how she looked, he contributed very little to the relationship. Rachel was expected to run errands and help James out on a regular basis, while James seemed blind to any of Rachel's needs. The two years she had been with him had been an emotional rollercoaster. There had been several break-ups and reunions within that time. Over the course of our discussions, she revealed that this was not the first man she had been with who was like this. In fact, two of her previous relationships had been with men who were arrogant, selfish and controlling. The ones who hadn't been like this she didn't feel as passionate about. I asked Rachel what first attracted her to James. "He's very good looking and successful and I thought he was gorgeous. He didn't seem selfish or arrogant when I first met him; in fact I loved the way he pursued me and how it made me feel." Rachel looked sad. "The negative traits only began to show themselves later on." She told me about her previous two boyfriends, and on the surface they were all quite different. One was a shy artist, and the other one worked in the world of finance. So I asked her if there was anything that attracted her in the beginning that they all had in common. "They all had a sexiness about them, and a certain cool aloofness that made them seem mysterious. I find that irresistible." I asked her what her father was like. Rachel gave me a sad smile. "Arrogant, selfish, controlling and aloof." What was Rachel's relationship like with her father? Not surprisingly, it was troubled. Rachel had learned to associate narcissistic behaviour with love from a very early age. It may have been painful, but there was also a comfort in being around the old familiar pattern. She had also learned that no matter what she did, it was never enough and yet, like a child, she kept on trying.

Becoming Conscious

Patterns are subconscious. They haven't been brought to our conscious awareness yet and that's why they keep happening. Why would our subconscious mind seek out someone who is just like someone in our past who hurt us? The Universe will keep presenting us with the same situation over and over again until we get the lesson and heal that part of ourselves. Once we have fully learned the lesson, we won't be attracted to the situation or the type of person again; in fact they won't even come into our energetic field. On a soul level we always seek healing. On an energetic level, Rachel was attracted to men with similar negative attributes to her father (even though they appeared different on the outside) and would continue to do so until she acknowledged the pattern and healed the wounds she carried. Therefore, it's important to acknowledge if there is a pattern in your choice of partner that isn't serving you, and to look back on previous painful relationships and ask yourself what the lessons were. Lessons are about you only, not the other person.

Equally important as our patterns of whom we choose, are our own patterns of behaviour. I asked Rachel about her own behaviour within the relationship.

She confided that once she realised James's faults, she decided to remain in the relationship, mistakenly thinking that if she was nice enough and kind enough and good enough, he would change. The only time change would happen, however, is when she left or threatened to leave, but it wouldn't last. Most of the time Rachel felt like she was walking on eggshells, being careful "not to upset him", and often swallowing her own anger in order to keep the peace. She came to realise that no matter what she did, he wouldn't change.

How did Rachel feel about her relationship with her father? She was still trying to win his approval and love, but it was forever elusive. I asked her what she thought the lesson in her love relationships might be. Rachel knew the answer. "To stop the pattern of being with people who can't or won't love me, and to stop trying to fix broken people. I can't fix them; they are the way they are, and if they can't love me properly, I need to let go and find real love." Rachel was able to walk away from James for good, and begin the process of releasing her pattern of choosing the wrong type of man and change her own behaviour in relationships. She also decided to meet with her father to tell him how she felt about their relationship. Not surprisingly, her father became defensive and told Rachel she was a disappointment to him. Rachel was calm throughout their exchange. "I think I can accept him for who he is, not for what I've hoped he would be, but I'm also going to protect myself by limiting future contact."

The healing journey wasn't over for Rachel. She continued to attract and be attracted to similar types of men. Each time she began a new relationship, the man she was seeing would begin to display similar traits. "Am I doomed for the rest of my life to attract these types of men?" she asked me, looking tired and exasperated. "No," I told her, remembering that the same thing had happened to me after I ended my relationship with the narcissist. "The Universe likes to test us a few times to ensure we've learned the lesson, that's all that's happening." With this new awareness, she was careful not to become sexually involved with anyone new too quickly. Whenever she felt an irrational, magnetic attraction, she learned to take a step back, observe his behaviours and create space before she took things any further. Rachel has since met and fallen in love with a man she is very happy with. If you know you are attracted to men who in the long run don't make you happy, it's important to take things slowly when dating someone new and not to become physically involved with him until you are quite sure who he is. You will need to learn how to ask him the right questions and to remain centred and grounded and not allow yourself to be swept off your feet by his charm. This will be discussed further in Step 5.

Steph came to see me because she had a pattern of choosing weak men. "I'm tired of being the strong one," she told me. Time and again, she would find herself with a man who was dependent on her in some way. Her ex-husband had been overly needy and expected her to bail him out of debt regularly; another boyfriend had had a drug problem and wanted her to save him. She now wasn't sure whether to end a relatively new relationship with a man she described as lazy, part-time employed and expecting her financial support. "Why are you helping him out financially?" I asked. She replied that she felt sorry for him and wanted to help him get on his feet. "Why would he bother when he has you to fall back on?" I asked. "Steph, you're going to have to change your behaviour. You've got to take responsibility for your part in this. Refuse to pay for anything else for him. Only then will he get the necessary lesson, and only then will you end your pattern of being with weak men. What are you afraid of?" I could see fear written all over her face as we spoke. "That he won't love me anymore and will leave." Steph believed that in order to keep a man, she had to be helping him, even if it meant she was denying her own financial security. Steph took my advice and stayed resolute about not giving her boyfriend money. The relationship was over within six weeks. Steph was devastated, but could see clearly that his so-called love was highly conditional. With her next relationship, she plans on having strong boundaries around how much she gives, and she plans on doing this from the outset.

Becoming conscious and breaking patterns is a process that unfolds in its own time. It is through our so-called relationship "mistakes" that we learn. The following poem by Portia Nelson describes the process perfectly:

I walk down the street.
There is a hole.
I don't see it.
I fall in.
It isn't my fault.
It takes a very long time to get out.

I walk down the same street.
There is still a deep hole.
I pretend not to see it.
I fall in.
I pretend it's not my fault.
It takes a long time to get out.

I walk down the same street.
There is still the same deep hole.
I see it.
I fall in anyway.
It's a habit.
I get out quicker this time.

I walk down the same street.
There is a deep hole.
I see it.
I walk around it.
I don't fall in.

I walk down a different street.

Change the way you think of previous relationships. Rather than seeing them as "failures", see them as necessary stepping-stones in your learning that have made you a better person.

Wanting to Rescue and Wanting to Be Rescued

Wanting to rescue or wanting to be rescued are two sides of the same coin. On a subconscious level, some women feel the need to rescue a man, while others feel the need to be rescued. The need to rescue will manifest in a pattern of choosing men who need to be "fixed" in some way, such as an addict, or a man with a myriad of problems. Women who rescue like feeling strong and having a challenge; the problem is that the challenges never end and this relationship pattern never brings happiness in the long run. Also known as co-dependents, these women only ever feel worthy and needed if they are helping or fixing someone. This takes their attention away from what they really need; to fix themselves.

Women who secretly hope that at some point they are going to be rescued by their Knight in Shining Armour will display a pattern of choosing men who are into power and control in relationships. A wish to be rescued can show up as someone who is not living their life to its full potential, in the hope that someone comes along and turns their life around. Someone often does, but not for the better. Eventually such a relationship will reveal a lack of fulfilment. These women live their partner's lives, but not their own. On a deep level, these women have low self-worth. They do not realise their own power, so look for it outside of themselves in the form of a man who promises them "the world".

It is important to let go of both myths. The only person who can rescue you is yourself. The only person who can rescue your partner is them.

The energy that we expend when we are constantly rescuing someone can be so much better spent on creating the life we want. I ask clients who are in "rescuing" relationships to imagine if all the energy they are expending on rescuing their partner were to be freed up. What could they do with it? Imagine the potential their life would have. I ask my clients who want to "be rescued", how could they rescue themselves? If they want to travel, why not do it? If they are in an unfulfilling job, why not take an evening course and re-educate in something they're passionate about? Why not develop their interests and expand themselves? Why not find out what their true potential is?

Following Your Head vs. Following Your Heart

People who follow their heart often believe in "love at first sight". This is a romantic notion that is not always a helpful one. While there can be "magnetic attraction" at first sight that can lead to a long-term fulfilling relationship, it can just as easily lead to a disastrous one if you are subconsciously attracted to the wrong type of man. Others will tell you that you should bypass the factors of physical attraction and chemistry and choose a partner with whom you share things in common, such as similar values, family background and interests. After all, companionship is highly necessary if you plan to spend your lives together. I believe that a combination of both is necessary for a fulfilling relationship. Physical attraction and chemistry are the glue that keeps a man and a woman together during difficult times. However, just as important is the rational consideration of whether your temperaments and view of the world fit well together, and that each other's circumstances are suitable. Therefore, in choosing a mate, a balance of both head and heart is needed.

Following your heart only can be disastrous, as Catherine, a successful lawyer, found out. She met Gerry, a policeman, and was strongly attracted by his masculinity, good looks and sense of justice. The sexual chemistry between them was electric and she told me she had never felt so in love. Their sexual relationship was passionate and fiery. All was not perfect, however. Gerry was divorced and had a bitter ex-wife. When his ex-wife found out he had a new relationship, she began denying Gerry access to his children. Gerry's moods began to swing. Catherine and Gerry didn't go out very often, as a good portion of his salary went to his ex-wife in child support. When they did go out, Catherine would pay. She was no longer enjoying the social life and lifestyle she had worked hard for, but felt that Gerry's love compensated for that. When she eventually met Gerry's children, they were rude and unaccepting of her. She and Gerry had talked about getting married, and Catherine told Gerry she wanted children in the future. Gerry was adamant he didn't want to have any more. She came to see me because she felt torn. Never had she felt such love and attraction for someone, yet his circumstances were going to be a challenge. I asked Catherine if she could foresee what the future held if she and Gerry were to commit. Catherine decided to stay in the relationship in the hope that the children might accept her, and that Gerry might change his mind about having more children. Neither of these eventuated. Catherine knew she needed to use her head and move on. No amount of love and passion were going to fix the problems looming in the future.

Following your head only can also lead to problems. Danni was married to George, and came to see me because she was in a terrible dilemma. She had met a man at work and felt a very strong attraction to him, so much so that she could no longer envision her future with George. She told me there had never been any "fireworks" with George, but they got on well together, shared similar interests and had a shared vision of the future. Committing to someone with whom we have little sexual chemistry is an accident waiting to happen. We are highly vulnerable to an affair of the heart in the future. Danni's dilemma remains unresolved.

Intimacy

Relationships, like all things, are not static. They involve change and movement. Over time, a couple's relationship will progress to deeper levels. The first phase of a relationship, which we refer to as "falling in love" is also known as infatuation or limerence. This phase feels exciting and sexually charged, but it doesn't last. When limerence begins to fade, we come back down to earth a little. Reality sets in as love's blindfolds are taken off and two people begin to see each other more realistically. A couple either "fall out of love" at this time or real love takes over. Real love involves a deeper sense of caring for the other person. Some people are addicted to limerence, and this is called "love addiction". Infatuation can feel like a drug, but it's not the kind of love that lasts. Love addicts feel constantly disappointed by relationships, in the false belief that the feelings of the early stages are supposed to last forever. During the next phase of a relationship, the couple move closer in a different way. They become more caring and intimate with each other. Intimacy is the ability to reveal our true selves to each other, to take off the masks we wear and become vulnerable. To do this, we must be able to trust. Some of us are more at ease with intimacy than others. For some, it could be likened to stepping over the edge of a cliff. If we want things to become deeper, we must risk showing our vulnerability. Intimacy builds upon itself. The more of ourselves we reveal our partner and he reveals to us, the more we understand and trust each other. This is what makes relationships special. A couple who are intimate are at ease with each other. If a relationship isn't created on intimacy, it has no true foundations. Some people are terrified of intimacy and are unable to take a relationship to the second level.

Sandy had been in a relationship with Colin for a year, and felt that it was going nowhere. When she endeavoured to open up a conversation about his inner thoughts or his hopes and dreams, Colin would shut down. Whenever things were going well, Colin would do something that would upset Sandy, such as start an argument, or cancel a date, or "go off the radar" by not phoning her for days. Colin's behaviour was typical of someone who was terrified of intimacy. He couldn't trust Sandy, or anyone, enough to get truly close and become vulnerable. Instead, whenever it appeared that they were getting too comfortable together, Colin would sabotage the relationship by doing something that would create distance between them. I explained to Sandy that Colin had an intimacy problem. Fear of intimacy is created from an old early wound that caused a lot of pain. On a subconscious level, a person decides that they never want to experience that pain again, and so will not get close to anyone. The only hope she had for Colin changing was for him to seek help. She asked Colin if he was willing to go for counselling, but he refused. Sandy ended the relationship, and has since found someone who is capable of "going over the edge".

Fear of intimacy is not to be confused with a need for space. We all have a need for intimacy as well as space. A need for space will show up as a man wanting to spend time with his friends, take time out to do things for himself on his own, or engage in a hobby or pastime that doesn't include his partner. This is normal and healthy, as long as it is interspersed with prolonged periods of intimacy with his partner.

Abandonment

Christine had a chronic problem. She had no problem meeting men, but no relationship would last longer than three months. "It's always exciting and passionate at first, and I feel so strong and sexy and powerful, and then they inevitably pull away. I become fearful that they're going to end it and they always do." I asked her what she did when she became fearful. "I tell them I know that something's changed. Then they pull away more and talk about how things aren't working. I find myself begging them to give it another chance." Christine's father walked out on the family when she was ten years old and she had been deeply affected by this. In relationships, she wanted to be wanted and desired (as she would have liked to feel as a young girl), and the "rush" of the first stage of a new relationship gave her this. When the relationship began to move to the second stage, her partner would begin to relax and not feel the need to "woo" her as much. Anyone with abandonment issues can begin to feel uncomfortable at this stage in a relationship, for this is when their inner security will be tested. As her partner began to feel more comfortable and relaxed, she would read this as him pulling away from her, and feel abandoned and fearful. She would react with needy behaviour that, for a relationship still in its infancy, can turn a partner off. The more she became needy, clingy and wanting to talk about "what was wrong", her partner would now want to genuinely pull away. Where had this wonderful, sexy, confident woman gone? When her partner attempted to end the relationship, Christine would become the abandoned ten-year-old girl, and plead with him to give it another chance. By this stage, he would be totally turned off by her insecurity and neediness and leave.

The beginning of a relationship is relatively easy – we show the best side of us and feel strong. We feel desirable because of the magic of limerence. The transition to intimacy can bring out the unhealed parts of us. I worked with Christine to excavate her abandonment issues and let go of the pattern of behaviour that had destroyed every potential relationship she had ever had. Issues around abandonment don't necessarily come from a physical abandonment; emotional abandonment at a young age will also leave its scars.

The Pattern of Abuse

It is a common misconception that abuse is either physical or verbal violence. While these are two significant kinds of abuse, there are many others. Abuse can be physical, emotional, psychological, verbal, sexual or financial. Abusers seek to control another person by intimidation or manipulation. If you have ever found yourself feeling afraid of a partner, it is likely the relationship was an abusive one. It's also important to ask yourself if your own behaviour is abusive, and if the answer is yes, it needs to be addressed. For treatment of abusive behaviours, I would suggest psychotherapy, NLP or kinesiology. Abuse is generally a long-term pattern of behaviour. Staying in an abusive relationship will eventually erode your sense of self-worth and self-confidence. Below is a brief description of the different kinds of abuse.

- **Physical Abuse** – behaviour ranging from throwing things and slamming doors, to shoving, hitting and kicking to bashing, choking or using a weapon.

- **Emotional/Psychological Abuse** – this type of abuse is more covert and involves creating an atmosphere of intimidation and uncertainty for the victim, by criticising, threatening, isolating and withholding affection and intimacy. Victims can feel that they are constantly walking on eggshells, or that they are "going crazy" because they cannot quite put their finger on what is wrong.

- **Verbal Abuse** – shouting, raging, name calling, blaming, accusing, berating, taunting, using put-downs, "joke" put-downs, interrogating or trivialising.

- **Sexual Abuse** – forcing sex on another, engaging in sex acts that the other person is not enjoying, or deliberately inflicting pain on another person during sex.

- **Financial Abuse** – stealing, controlling another person's economic means, not allowing a partner to take part in financial decisions, or preventing a partner from having a job.

Sally is an attractive 48-year-old doctor and the mother of four children. She is now divorced from her ex-husband. My heart went out to her as I heard the story of her marriage. While they appeared the perfect family on the outside, Sally had endured years of emotional, verbal, financial and sexual abuse. "He never hit me," she told me, but the wounds he inflicted were probably more terrible. Her ex-husband had been incapable of true intimacy. The sex he preferred was cold and kinky. When things didn't go his way, he would inflict long, withdrawn silences on the family, during which Sally and the children felt they were walking on eggshells. This is a form of "passive" emotional abuse. Her husband wanted to control Sally. He fired the nanny, so that she would have to stop working at her job, he closed their joint bank account without telling her so that Sally wasn't able to withdraw money on her own, and he banned Sally's friends from coming to the house. Sally had a breakdown at the age of 43 and her husband had her committed to a mental ward. Sally had grown up believing in strong family values, and in keeping the family together, but in deciding to stay with this man, she had paid a huge price – her mental health. She did, however, find the emotional and mental strength to divorce him, and after several years of court battles, is now rebuilding her life. Sally will never be entirely free of him as he is the father of their four children. I relate this story to anyone who is in a relationship with an abusive person. Do not try to fix him, and do not hope that one day he will change. Run!

There are many reasons why women enter into relationships with men who are abusive. It may be a family pattern, low self-esteem or because an abuser can be charming at first, telling a woman what she wants to hear. Many abusers are manipulative and know how to go about getting what they want. However, an abuser's true colours usually begin to emerge at least several months after a couple have been together. By the time this has happened, a woman will already be emotionally invested in the relationship and choose to stay, hoping he will change back to the charming man he was at first. This is unlikely to happen, because the couple will get stuck in the cycle of abuse, whereby the relationship goes through very specific phases. It begins with the relationship going well, then the abuser begins to voice or display discontent and there is a build-up of tension. During this phase, the victim may feel like they're walking on eggshells. The abuser then unleashes the abuse. Afterwards he may be contrite, promising he will never do it again. The victim forgives him, hoping this is a new beginning. This is followed by the honeymoon period where the couple feel reunited and in love again, but it doesn't last. Before long, there is a build-up of tension, and on it goes. The pattern continues unless there is professional intervention, and even then it's going to be a long road before the abuser can or will change. Some women may convince themselves that they will be the woman who finally changes him. He may even tell her this, and she might feel flattered that she is so "good for him" (ignoring the fact that he's not good for her). Many women stay, convinced that it's their own fault and if only they did this or that he wouldn't be like this. Some stay for financial reasons while others stay simply because they have lost all self-esteem and self-confidence, and cannot envision a different future or any other possibilities. That is why it's important to take your time to get to know someone before committing.

Why is it that "nice" women who want to please tend to be attracted to angry, abusive men and vice versa? Because abusive men want women who they can control and dominate, and "nice" women feel they need a strong, assertive man. Rarely do you see abusive men go for a "bitch". This is another reason for women to embrace their shadow – the "bitch" is a necessary part of our personality. She is strong and protects us, nullifying the need for someone outside of ourselves to protect us.

Women with a strong need to please are just as dysfunctional as the abusive male. They hope that by pleasing others around them, they will find happiness. While it's true that giving is within our true spiritual nature, giving solely for the purpose of pleasing another at the expense of our own values and needs, is not healthy. In this relationship, unless one party decides to get help and change, they will be forever stuck in a pattern, each feeding off the other.

Men to Avoid

There are men with certain characteristics who should be avoided at all costs if you want a functional, happy long-term relationship. It is highly unlikely that any amount of your love or goodwill will change them. Here I have listed nine types, and while I don't like the use of labels, it can be useful for the purpose of identifying those who are not capable of a fulfilling long-term relationship. Each category is not mutually exclusive. You may find that a man who fits one of these descriptions may fit at least another as well. Some of these "types" will also be an abuser.

Men to Avoid at All Costs

1.   **The Sociopath** – This man has no conscience whatsoever, but he is highly intelligent. Unfortunately he uses his intelligence in the worst way possible. Sociopaths like women who are financially well off, will use them for their money, and leave when it suits them. In particular they like to choose widows and divorcees, manipulating them into spending money on things the sociopath wants, in the guise that it's "for us". Sociopaths are the ultimate "users".

Early signs he may be a sociopath: He will sweep you off your feet at first with his charming, charismatic personality, he may name-drop and talk himself up with his poetic use of words, and talk about business deals that there is no evidence of. He may not have any money of his own, will ask you for loans or want you to invest your money in his "business scheme". He may also indulge in irrational, spontaneous and risky behaviour that most of us wouldn't.

2.   **The Narcissist** – He's self-centred and has little or no empathy for others. If he doesn't get what he wants, he's likely to rage at you or go into long silences. You will be ignored if he's getting attention from elsewhere and he'll treat you like a doormat and then resent you for being one.

Early signs he may be a narcissist: He may seem too good to be true, sweeping you off your feet with his overly magnetic personality. He loves everything that you love and will make big promises. When the mask begins to slip, he will no longer love everything you love and may deny ever saying he did, will not follow through on the promises, will want to have things his own way, will speak badly of exes and may refer to them as "crazy", and blame others, and eventually you, for everything.

Men to Avoid if You Possibly Can

The following types are also not good relationship material, although if they are willing to address their issues and get help, you may have a slim chance of a lasting relationship. Personally, I would prefer to avoid them, and save myself a lot of time, energy and heartache.

3. **The Player** – This man sees the art of picking up women and romancing them as a game, and is always looking for the next best thing. It's only a matter of time before he's unfaithful to you. It is unlikely you will ever be able to trust him.

Early signs he may be a player: He is bold, confident and smooth. He may reveal his feelings for you a little too soon, and take you on overly romantic dates. He tends to have few solid friends because his life is lived at a superficial level, and he may be interested in thrill-seeking activities because he's bored when he's not being challenged.

4.   **The Committaphobe** – He's been a bachelor for a long time, and will tell you that he just hasn't found the right woman. He'll sweep you off your feet and you'll think you're the one he's been looking for his whole life. That is, until you suggest he meets your family or you talk about the future. Watch the backtracking begin. This man has a very deep fear of commitment, so when he begins to see your human faults, he'll use that as an excuse to run.

Early signs he may be a committaphobe: He's had many brief relationships, and perhaps some longer ones that are either long-distance or with unavailable people. He will be charming at first, knowing this will be an intense but short-lived relationship, and attempt to slow things down once he knows he's got you.

5.   **The Addict** – Whether it's alcohol, drugs, gambling, sex, porn or work, the addiction will be loved more than you. Such a relationship usually turns into an emotional rollercoaster of pain. If you're the child of an addict, be aware that you are particularly vulnerable to being attracted to an addict.

Early signs he may be an addict: This is a very brief overview, but each addiction eventually leads to fractured relationships.

Alcohol – established pattern of heavy drinking, behaviour changes when drinking, withdrawal symptoms when not drinking.

Drugs – low motivation and concentration, insomnia and agitation, disappears without explanation.

Gambling – frequents gambling establishments, mood swings, excessive amounts of money spent on gambling, will bet even after a significant windfall or loss.

Sex – sex dominates his life to the exclusion of other activities, multiple partners or cheating, habitual masturbation, may indulge in phone sex, computer sex, prostitutes, porn or exhibitionism, focuses on act of sex as opposed to connection between two people.

Porn – spends a lot of time on the internet, sexually unresponsive and not fully present with you, secretive behaviour.

Work – works long hours, seeks approval and acceptance through work, sees work as an escape from everyday problems, overly concerned with image, has control issues and is a perfectionist with himself and possibly others.

6. **The Control Freak** – At first you'll think it's great that he wants to spend all his time with you, but it's not so great when he starts telling you what you should wear, what friends you're allowed to see and how you are supposed to think and feel. A control freak sees you as an extension of him, and will endeavour to manipulate you in order to get his own way.

Early signs he may be a control freak: In the beginning, he will want to dictate where you go and when. A little later he'll start asking a lot of questions like "Where were you?", "Who were you with?", will try and drive a wedge between you and your family and friends by saying negative things about them so as to isolate you and have better control of you, will give you "guilt trips" when you want to do something he doesn't want you to do.

7. **The Victim** – He won't take responsibility for himself and realise his own power, and as a result his life is out of control. He complains about many things, but does nothing to help himself or the situation. If he's not already, he will end up bitter and angry. Victims sabotage themselves and then blame others for it.

Early signs he may be a victim: He blames other people, things and circumstances for what's not gone well in his life, has a "what's the use?" attitude when you suggest ways to help, passive or overt anger.

8. **The Mama's Boy** – If he's close to his mother and he puts her before you, beware. If he is still living with his mother, be even more aware. We are meant to break away from our parents as we turn into young adults. If a man is still overly attached to his mother and idolising her by the time he is in his late 20's, it's unlikely he's going to break that special connection and you are unlikely to ever measure up. His mother will also be

idolising him, and you will be considered an unwanted intruder.

Early signs he's a mama's boy: He won't live far from his mother, will talk about her a lot and compare you to her. Later on, any plans he makes with you will be dependent upon how it fits in with his mother or family. If you disagree with his mother, he'll take her side.

9. The Unavailable Man

A man who is already married or in a committed long-term relationship – the majority of married men who have affairs do not leave their wives. Some do, but most women don't realise what they're in for if he does. You will be tagged as "the other woman" for a long time and his ex-wife and possibly his children may revile you. Be prepared to be supportive during his divorce and settlement process because the man you found so alluring in the beginning may become a stressed-out wreck for a long period. He may not stay with you even if he does leave his wife, and whether he does or not, the beginning of your relationship will probably be tainted by grief, loss and conflict. I have counselled several women who married men they had affairs with. These women were struggling with feelings of either guilt or mistrust further down the track.

A man just out of a marriage or long-term relationship – while many men jump into a new relationship not long after a significant break-up, they are often not ready for another long-term commitment. A woman who has a relationship with a recently separated man is termed the "transition person" when it doesn't last. Many men cannot face being on their own and will seek out a new relationship as soon as their marriage is over, without being aware that they're not ready. There are few early signs that he isn't ready for a relationship, so beware of anyone who has recently become single from a long-term commitment.

Jenny and Peter worked together and they had always gotten on well. When Peter's marriage of 25 years ended, he asked Jenny out on a date. The friendship quickly turned to passionate romance. "Peter told me he realised that we were meant to be together," said Jenny. A few months later, Peter was facing the reality of divorce, a court settlement and difficulties in his relationships with his grown up children. Jenny did her best to keep Peter feeling upbeat, she listened to his troubles, organised romantic weekends away and began to forge good relationships with his adult children. When Peter finally completed his financial settlement with his ex-wife a year after he and Jenny had been together, he announced that he "needed space" and now wasn't sure what he wanted in the future. Jenny was stunned. This felt so unfair. She had supported Peter in his darkest hours and now that his life was looking more clear and certain, he wasn't sure whether he wanted to be with her. Peter went on an overseas sailing trip for three months without Jenny and when he came back he ended their relationship. In hindsight, Jenny could see that their union was doomed from the start.

Peter wasn't ready to settle down again immediately after a divorce, even though he thought he did at the time. Divorce is a process, and an unknown one for those going through it for the first time. Most divorcees feel a sudden sense of freedom when their divorce is through, and in particular when their financial settlement is complete, because their material ties with the ex-spouse are cut, setting them free. I asked Jenny to look back and reflect on any early warning signs in the relationship. "I was wary he was just out of a marriage, and that it may be too soon, but he seemed so sure, and I felt afraid that if I didn't take him up on it, I'd miss the opportunity of finally having the relationship I'd wanted. I guess it just wasn't meant to be". A person whose divorce and settlement is complete is going to be more ready for a commitment, than someone who is in the process of divorce and settlement.

❧

Exercise 6

Learning from Past Relationships

This can be a long exercise and can be emotionally draining, so choose a time when you have a few hours to yourself.

If you have past relationship experiences that hurt you, do this writing exercise in your journal for each one of these relationships. Past toxic relationships may include previous partners, parents, or anyone who has been abusive or hurtful to you.

- Write down all the hurts you are carrying from your relationship with this person (ie. Everything you feel they did that wronged you). Don't confuse this with negative thinking. On a therapeutic level, it's good to get all of this out and onto paper. Write down everything you can possibly think of. You don't want to be carrying this anymore.

- Now write down what you felt. Acknowledge all the feelings that come up in you over these past hurts and write down the words that express that feeling (humiliated, angry, deeply hurt, sad).

• Write down what you would do differently in the future (I would set the limits early on, I would say no if asked for a loan, I would walk away sooner). This is taking responsibility, owning your part in the relationship and acknowledging that you have personal power.

• Finally, write down all the lessons you learned from this relationship (I learned that just because a man is good looking and successful it doesn't make him good partner material, I learned that being around controlling people won't ever allow me to truly shine, I learned that the only person I can change is myself).

∽

For much of my life, I had a pattern of being attracted to men who were powerful, controlling and angry, while I took on the role of the pleaser and rescuer. I was blind to this pattern until I began therapy and acknowledged that as a child I took on a pleaser/rescuer role in my family. Whatever role we play in our family of origin we bring into our adult relationships. What I hadn't realised as an adult is that I had all the power I needed within myself, and so I looked for it in the men I chose. Having not dealt with the issue before, I left my powerful, controlling husband for someone whose need for power and control was insatiable. I had a two year intensive lesson in what narcissism is. I can now thank that person for the more important lesson beyond the two years of misery I put myself through. All that we need and desire is within ourselves, and we will never find happiness by seeking a missing part of ourselves in another.

Forgiveness

Have you forgiven people in your past who have hurt you? Not forgiving is like an energetic block that will harden you and make you less open to love. Carrying feelings of hatred and revenge is like swallowing poison and expecting the other person to die. Forgiving means acknowledging what the other person did to you, letting it go and not wasting your energy any longer on hating or wanting revenge. It doesn't mean that this person is invited back into your life in any way; in fact it's best if they don't come back into your life, in order for you to fully move on. The only person who will benefit from your forgiveness is you. The other person probably wouldn't care less whether you've forgiven them or not. When you forgive, you let go of the energetic blocks that will become emotional baggage that drains your energy and sabotages future relationships. By forgiving, you free up energy, which can be put into areas of your life that are worthwhile.

Forgiveness can be a process. Sometimes we're not ready to forgive, particularly if it's a recent hurt. We may need to process everything that happened before we are ready. That's okay, but I do suggest to my clients, when they are ready, that in order to forgive and rid themselves of any grudges, the first step is to send the person unconditional love. This may feel repellent, but if you can see the love you're sending as the Universe's unconditional love, not your love, it makes it easier and will fast-track the process of letting go of any negative energy that is poisoning you. Another way to allow yourself to forgive is to de-personalise what they did to you, by accepting that this is how that person, at their level of evolution, operates in the world. It just happened to be you on the other end of it, but it could have been someone else.

In my own case, I decided to leave my narcissistic boyfriend, who then endeavoured to destroy my financial stability, my friendships and my reputation. My ex-husband was still angry at me and aimed to punish me in whatever way he could as well. I realised he would probably never forgive me for leaving him. I had certainly got my karma! For some time I felt fearful of both of them. I knew I had to release myself energetically from both men. Accepting them for who they were made it easier for me to forgive them.

Forgiving our Parents

At some point in our lives, most of us have to forgive our parents for not measuring up or letting us down, particularly when we begin the journey of excavating our beliefs and past patterns and realise that many can be attributed to our parents. This can lead to feelings of anger towards our parents. However, the truth is that most of us were loved by our parents; our parents just didn't have the awareness and skills that were needed, because they were blindly following their subconscious beliefs, handed down from their own parents. When we can accept that our parents did the best job they could with the knowledge and skills they had, we are able to forgive them.

In the Bible, God says he will "punish the children for the sins of the fathers to the third and fourth generation of those who hate me, but show love to 1,000 of those who love me and keep my commandments". In other words, if we continue with old dysfunctional patterns, we will be condemned to experience the same mistakes as our parents, but if we can rise above our old incorrect family patterns and live our truth, we will live blessed lives. It is our responsibility in this lifetime to break the old patterns that no longer serve us.

❧

Exercise 7

Forgiveness

Do this exercise for every person you need to forgive.

- Sit quietly in a chair and close your eyes. Picture that person. Say that person's name (to yourself is fine) and then say:

- "I forgive you for all the things you did to me. I take in all the lessons I was meant to learn from my association with you."

- Give yourself a moment to reflect on lessons you have gained from this relationship. Lessons should be about you, not the other person, and should be positive. (I learned that being around someone who is dishonest is not good for my self-esteem and self-worth and I deserve honesty in a relationship, I learned that I can't fix another person).

- After you have reflected on your lessons, say:

- "I live in the present and refuse to dwell on past people and past circumstances. I let you go with love."

- Now picture a cord that connects you both. Visualise cutting that cord and watch that person float away into the light.

If this is a person you find yourself dwelling on a lot, do this exercise every day for a few weeks. You will be surprised by how differently you will feel within a short time.

❦

When we forgive, our energy changes. We become lighter, emotionally freer and far more open to love. Remember, like attracts like. If you're sending out a loving, clear energy, you'll be attracting in loving, clear energy.

Addressing Our Own Behaviour

It is easy to point the finger at the other person if things haven't worked out, but it is necessary to address and own our part in a relationship. We all have patterns of behaviour – some that serve us and some that don't. Reflect on your own behaviour in relationships. Do you re-enact certain behaviours? It's wonderful if they enable the relationship to grow and prosper, but if you suspect your actions have damaged previous relationships, it's time to address them. If you're unsure why you keep repeating a negative behavioural trait, I would suggest counselling or kinesiology to excavate the source and the reason for the behaviour.

Belinda's last relationship ended because of her uncontrollable anger and jealousy and it wasn't the first time a relationship had ended because of it. She had now met Nick and the old pattern was re-appearing. She came to see me because she didn't want to sabotage this relationship. During the course of therapy, Belinda revealed that she had had angry outbursts since childhood. Belinda told me that when her mother remarried when she was ten, and her attention withdrew from her and became focused on her new husband, she had felt emotionally abandoned. Whenever Nick spent time away from her or gave his attention to others, she felt jealous, threatened and angry. By creating awareness around her abandonment, and owning it as "her issue", not her partner's, Belinda was able to see that what was happening wasn't the problem; how she chose to see the event was creating her anger. In Belinda's case, whenever her relationships felt threatened, she would become the ten year old who felt abandoned.. Old emotional triggers can be deeply ingrained. At a subconscious level, Belinda's belief was "If I love, I get abandoned". I worked with Belinda to find a more realistic belief to replace the old one. She replaced it with "I love and I am safe". There is no guarantee for any of us that love will last; all we can do is give our relationships our best. I asked her to appreciate that even though earlier relationships hadn't worked out, she had survived and now had another chance with Nick. Emotions based on fear such as anger and jealousy will never allow a relationship to flourish, so Belinda created another affirmation. "I allow Nick and myself space to enjoy our friendships". Now, whenever Belinda feels her fear and anger triggered, she takes a deep breath and allows space before reacting in any way. She honours the childhood wound she carries and focuses on being a fully present adult in the current situation.

Underneath a recurring pattern of anger is childhood grief. Talking therapy alone is unlikely to heal chronic anger. Psychotherapy that includes psychodrama, NLP and kinesiology are effective ways of healing anger.

Self-Forgiveness

Are you ashamed of any actions from your past, such as betraying another person or acting in a way that hurt another person? Unless you have acknowledged the lesson and forgiven yourself for these past actions, you may be carrying an energetic block of guilt and shame. These emotions can create a subconscious belief that you aren't worthy or deserving of love in the future. In order to expect the best in the future, we must forgive ourselves. Self-forgiveness is just as important as forgiving others. If we want to have a loving relationship with ourselves, we must let go of past actions that we don't feel good about.

Here I will share with you another part of my story. For a very long time, I carried with me a deep sense of shame for hurting my ex-husband and my children. I felt I didn't deserve happiness, having destroyed the happiness of those close to me. Even though I had made amends with my children, I struggled to forgive myself and to truly move on with my life. It was during a counselling session that my wonderful counselling teacher, Jane, made me aware of the guilt and shame that I was carrying around with me, and how I was sabotaging my life with it. She asked me to acknowledge that although I had made a mistake, it wasn't all my fault. I had been emotionally neglected for many years and was vulnerable to the attentions of someone else. She asked me to acknowledge my "humanness". Being human means that we don't always make wise choices; often we make choices based on an immediate need without giving thought to the consequences. This didn't make me a "bad" person. By forgiving myself I would be doing those I loved a huge service, as we are meant to live life to our full potential. She then took me through this beautiful exercise below.

❧

Exercise 8

Self-Forgiveness

Sit quietly in a chair and close your eyes. Imagine your Higher Self (the spiritual part of you that is connected to the Divine) standing behind and above you. Your Higher Self is looking down on you with pure, unconditional love. Your Higher Self knows that you are here on Earth to learn lessons through experience and there is no wrong or right, just that which serves you or does not serve you. Acknowledge the lessons you have learned through your perceived mistake. Your Higher Self loves you, no matter what you have done and is forgiving you for all the choices you have made that have left you with feelings of guilt or shame. Imagine the negative emotions of guilt and shame exiting out through your arms and legs, freeing you of any negative feelings towards yourself.

❧

I found this exercise to be very powerful. Having let go of my guilt and shame, I began to realise that I, too, deserved happiness and a wonderful life.

STEP FOUR

CLARIFY WHAT IT IS YOU WANT

Become clear on your desires and set your goals

"Imagination is everything. It is the preview of life's coming attractions."
- Albert Einstein

Having learned your lessons of the past and being willing to break any negative patterns, it is time to establish your goals. Many people go through life uncertain of what it is they want, and as a result, their lives are lived by default. By defining what it is you want in a relationship and in a partner, you are setting a goal. The Universe wants to give you what you want and the more precise you are with that information, the more precise the result will be. If you want a relationship, define what that is.

A good relationship goes well beyond the first spark of infatuation, and takes time to mature into a deep connection that is based on true intimacy, honesty, respect, friendship and good communication. It requires both partners to accept each other exactly as they are, not as how they would like them to be. While there is no such thing as perfection, we need to find someone who is willing to meet our needs, and whose needs we are willing to meet. Good relationships are a paradox. They must feel easy and free, yet they take commitment and effort. A successful relationship requires each partner to support and honour the choices of the other and encourage their personal growth, and yet it also requires that each partner surrender to become "we" rather than "I". Good relationships require a balance of both closeness and space. Each partner needs to honour the other's personal boundaries but also have the capacity to become close and "as one". This must be something we aspire to, and it will take two people who are willing to grow, learn and evolve and accept that there will be challenges.

An authentic relationship is not about how it looks on the outside; it's about what's really happening on the inside. I have met women who are obsessed about the idea of marriage, an engagement ring, the big wedding, buying the perfect house and "living the dream". While these are all lovely trimmings, they are not the relationship.

Values

For goals to be sound, we must base them on our values. Values are the foundation from which we build our life. What is it you value? If you're not sure, complete the following exercise.

❦

Exercise 9

What are My Values?

- **Write down the names of five people you most admire. They may be someone you know or a well-known person.**

- **Now, beside each name, write down the qualities in them that you most admire (kindness, love, wisdom, success, wealth, fitness, presence, strength, humour, beauty, resilience, helpfulness, creativity).**

- **Look through your answers. The words you have written down will be your most important values.**

- **Next, write a list of your values based on your answers. Here's an example.**

- o **Love**

- o **Financial security**

- o **Career success**

- o **Helping others**

- o **Being in nature**

- o **Staying fit and attractive**

- o **Feeling balanced**

- o **Family**

- **Now list them in order of priority.**

❧

Values provide a framework by which we can create our goals and make wise decisions that lead to personal fulfilment. Goals that go against our values are unlikely to be attained, as they won't fit into the 'ecology' of our lives. For example, if you have a goal that you would like to meet your life partner, buy a house, settle down and have a family, but your values are based on freedom, adventure and travel, it is unlikely that you will attract the outcome to you, unless your values change.

Be Specific in Your Goals

What kind of relationship do you want? Is it marriage? Does it include children? Is it a live-in partner without a formal commitment? Is it someone you go out with but don't live with? I ask this question, because many people do not define what the relationship they want will look like. I have counselled women who think they would like a committed long-term relationship, but on a subconscious level, they don't.

Adrienne said she knew what she wanted. She had made a specific list of all the qualities she required in a partner, and wanted to get married and have children. However, each boyfriend she dated had almost none of the qualities she had listed, and each relationship would end after a few months. "Why are you going out with him?" I challenged her. "You told me you wanted to find a man who hasn't got children and is kind and honest!" Adrienne was actually sabotaging her own happiness because, on a deeper level, she was frightened of intimacy.

What qualities do you want your partner to have? Look back over your past. What have you learned? What don't you want? Most women I meet are more than willing to tell me what they don't want, but fail to specify what it is they do want. What do you want? The more specific you are, the more the Universe can help you.

Here are some qualities that are essential in a partner if you want a happy long-term relationship.

1.   **Openness, honesty and integrity** – Dishonesty doesn't always come in the form of lies – it can show up as secrecy or silence. People who have nothing to hide are transparent in their actions and words. When their actions match their words, they have integrity.

2.   **Empathy and kindness** – Empathy is the ability to feel what another is feeling. Being in sync with another's feelings will naturally lead to kindness. Those with an inability to empathise are not only cold and unfeeling, but often cruel.

3.   **Generosity** – A person with a willingness to share and give of their time, energy and things will make constant investments in a relationship.

4.   **Self sufficiency** – When a person is capable of supporting themselves on a financial and physical level, they are ready for the responsibility of a committed relationship, and not before.

5.   **A Willingness to Learn and Grow** – Being able to take constructive criticism and work on areas of personal development that are needed will be necessary in a long term relationship. Refusing to transform will not enable a relationship to grow.

Without the above qualities, no relationship will stand the test of time. Read the list again, and ask yourself how you rate in each of these areas. Is there an area you need to work on?

After my divorce and subsequent relationship, I wrote a wish list based on all the relationship lessons I had learned. No longer did I want a man who was into power and control. I wanted to be with someone who treated me as his equal. By being specific about all the qualities that would be important in a partner for me, I not only attracted a totally different type of man; I broke a destructive pattern.

∽

Exercise 10

The Wish List

Keeping in mind the above list of qualities as essentials, make a list of the extra qualities you would like in a partner. Here's an example:

- **Sense of humour**
- **Loving and affectionate**
- **Financially stable**
- **Attractive**
- **Fit**

- Adventurous – likes to travel
- Lives in the same city as me

Add as much to this list as you feel is important to you. When you have finished the list, rank each quality in importance. As you look at your list, ask yourself how you rate in each of these characteristics. Are there any areas where you would consider yourself lacking? If so, ask yourself why you need a partner with this particular quality. Are you hoping that he will make up for something you don't have? For example, if you want a man who is fit and you're a couch potato, you may be hoping that your partner will motivate you and that their self-discipline may rub off on you. It's time to start getting motivated to get fit on your own. Are you looking for a man who's financially well off, but you're struggling financially? It's time to look at rescuing yourself from financial hardship. Looking for someone who is going to make up for your weaknesses isn't a good foundation. The good news is, through this exercise, you have gained awareness of where you need to do some personal development. Focus on improving this area of your life, not on finding a mate to fix it.

Now run your wish list past your list of values. Are there any clashes? If so, reflect on why that is and make the appropriate adjustments to your wish list.

❧

Use Your Imagination

Do you remember being a child and letting your imagination run wild? Allow yourself to be that child again. Now that you have clarity about what it is you want in a partner, it is time to use your imagination. Imagine this person in your life. When you have a clear vision of your future dream, run movies in your mind of situations you desire, such as activities you would like to do with him, places you would like to go, the home you would live in together, your wedding if that is what you want, your first child together. Let your imagination go wild! Imagine until you feel it's real, and a feeling of joy and "having" comes over you. Some people may call this wishful thinking, and it is. You are thinking about what you wish for and when you take the time to imagine the things you desire, you are in the process of attracting it to you. Make your imaginings even more real by using all of your senses - add sounds, smells and tastes. Allow your imagination to take you to a blissful place whenever you have free time – before or after a meditation, riding the bus, walking while listening to your favourite music, and do so until it feels real.

Detachment

Once you have presented your dream to the Universe by imagining it, detach from it with the certainty that the desire will be fulfilled. Positive feelings of happiness and joy raise your vibration to the frequency of receiving. Negative feelings block the energetic flow and your desire won't come to you. Make time every day to daydream and envision your future relationship in as much detail as possible, but do not allow in negative thoughts about not having it now. Instead, enjoy the journey from now on; knowing you will have what it is you want in divine and perfect timing. Divine and perfect timing is not *your* timing. It is important to allow the Universe the time to create for you what it is you want, and have faith that it is on its way when the time is right.

Finding myself single at 47 and having faced my loneliness and forgiven myself, a wonderful thing happened. I began to change how I saw my life. I wasn't a sad, lonely 47-year-old divorcee. I was a totally free woman whose life lay before her like a huge blank canvas just waiting to be painted on. I was at the halfway point in my life. What would I like to achieve in the second half of my life? I wrote down a list of goals. Among these goals was "Love". I created a vision board – a visual depiction of everything I wanted. To represent "Love", I glued a picture I found in a magazine of a man and a woman holding hands walking along a beach, because the beach is a very special place for me. I created an affirmation: "I trust true love to find me in divine and perfect timing". Recently I retrieved my vision board, now three years old, from a corner of my study and a heavy wave of emotion swept over me. Not only had I achieved nearly everything I put on that vision board; I had found love... And I had met my partner on the beach!

∽

Exercise 11

Picture Your Future on Your Timeline

Look at your wish list. Visualise putting your wish into a gift box, and wrap it up. Sit quietly and picture the timeline of your life. Step onto the **NOW** and float above it. Look towards your future, and float to a point on the timeline where your dream will be realised. Drop your gift box on that point on the timeline. As you float above this event, look back towards the **NOW** and notice all the points along the way that have led to this happy event. These points represent periods of personal growth, positive changes you made to your life, new friendships and social circles and "coincidences". Appreciate the rich journey you have been on to get to this point in the future. Now float back to **NOW**, and feel joyful and confident about the future, knowing that your

dream can become a reality and that you can enjoy every moment of the journey between NOW and when you meet your ideal partner.

❧

Now that you have put your goal out there to the Universe, relax and accept that it will come to you in Divine Universal Timing. In the meantime, get on with living a joyful, purposeful and rich life.

Gratitude

In order to be in the positive Universal flow, focus on being grateful for what you have. Focusing on what we don't have, and feeling negative about it, is what so many of us do. We can be so busy noticing our problems that we fail to see the good things in our lives. When we focus on problems, the Universe answers us with more problems. When we put our attention on what we have and feel genuine gratitude for these things, the Universe gives us more to be grateful for. Get into the habit every day of keeping a Gratitude Journal. Even if you think your life isn't going well, there are always things to be grateful for. You can start with the smallest things: a good cup of coffee, a friendly chat at work, the feel of your sheets as you drift off to sleep, a sunny day, a flower you see. So many people walk through life blind to its beauty and all it has to offer. This is true poverty. The more you practise gratitude, the more things, people, opportunities and love will present themselves to you because you are opening your eyes to the Universe's endless gifts. We live in an abundant Universe, and the more we open up to this belief, the more abundance will be given to us.

Staying on Track

There will be times when you are going to get disheartened. Disappointment when we realise that a potential relationship is not going to work out or when someone lets us down, occasions such as Christmas or a wedding when we may suddenly feel the emptiness of having no partner in our lives. The negative feelings of fear, hopelessness and sadness can easily arise at these times, and plunge us into a negative energy vibration. When this does happen, it's important to acknowledge the feelings that come up and honour them by allowing yourself to feel them. However, you don't need to remain in a negative state for too long. In NLP, we say that "there is no such thing as failure; only feedback". Almost every successful person in the world has had to experience failure before they have experienced success. These words by the basket-baller Michael Jordan tell it as it is:

"I've missed more than 9,000 shots in my career. I've lost almost 300 games. 26 times I've tried to take the game winning shot and missed. I've failed over and over and over again in my life. And that is why I succeed."

The following exercise will lift you out of a negative state, and bring you back into the positive Universal flow.

∽

Exercise 12

Getting Back into the Universal Flow

Stand in a room where you have some space in front of you. This is a stepping exercise where you will be stepping forward four times.

• Step 1 – As you stand in the first position, acknowledge your feelings of disheartenment and disappointment. Adapt the physiology that represents the way you feel (round shoulders, sad face).

• Step 2 – Step forward into the second position. In this space, acknowledge that there is a far bigger picture than you will ever understand and that everything happens for a reason. This space represents the mystery of the Universe. Close your eyes and be in the "nothingness" of the Universe and detach from your negative feelings. As you do this, open your body and breathe in deeply.

• **Step 3** – Step forward into the third position. In this space, recall your hopes, desires and wishes. Imagine having them. Adapt the physiology of how you will feel when you have these things (standing tall, smile).

• **Step 4** – Step forward into the fourth position. Ask yourself what is it that you can do or give to yourself right now that will contribute to your desired outcome (this can be anything that helps you feel good such as meditate, go for a walk, have a massage, have a manicure, do a creative project, read a helpful book, call a friend, be in nature).

• **Step 5** – Step forward into the fifth position. This position says "Action". Adapt the physiology of taking action (standing tall, stepping forward).

This exercise allows you to work through and process negative emotions and gets you back on track in a short period of time.

৶

Maintaining a Positive Attitude

Here are some ways of maintaining a positive attitude:

- Look through your wish list every day, and imagine your ideal partner in your future, to the point where you feel you actually have it.

- Create a vision board using pictures, words and anything else you feel would represent your future relationship with your ideal partner, (words such as love, companionship, connection, pictures representing your desired future such as the house you would like to live in, the holidays you would like to have with him, a man with the kind of looks that appeal to you, a ring if you want marriage, a child if you want to have children). Display the vision board where it is in your line of vision every day. Even if you don't consciously look at it, your subconscious mind will be registering it and co-operating with the Universe to find it for you.

- Signs around your home also help you maintain a positive attitude. Some suggested phrases for your signs are:

    o I can do it

    o Stay determined

    o Never give up

o "Go confidently in the direction of your dreams" (Thoreau)

o "When you are going through hell, keep going" (Winston Churchill)

o "This too shall pass".

STEP FIVE

MAKE WISE CHOICES IN THE PRESENT

Learn to be happy, present and true to yourself

"As within, so without"
- *Hermessianex, Greek Poet*

You have now begun the process of internal change, and from this will naturally come external changes. Through pro-actively loving yourself, you will gain good self-esteem. With a higher self-esteem, you will make wiser choices and be willing to be alone when the need arises. Through taking responsibility for your life to date and changing your beliefs and patterns where necessary, you can change your behaviour and alter the course of your life. By believing in abundance and possibilities, not scarcity and hopelessness, you open yourself up to the universal flow. And by becoming clear and setting goals, you can attract into your life all that you want.

In order to create the right conditions for manifesting a relationship, imagine that you will never meet your future love. If this were the case, how would you choose to live your life? Would you be working in the career you're in now, or would you be doing something different? Would you be investing more in your current friendships? Would you be pursuing your personal interests and goals more? Filling our lives with all that we desire and discovering our full potential is what we are meant to do. Make your own fulfilment your number one priority.

Happiness

"I'm so unhappy because it didn't work out," said Carla, after three months of dating Oliver. "Have you ever considered that you can choose happiness even when things haven't gone the way you wanted them to?" Carla looked puzzled. "Happiness is a choice," I explained. "I discovered this when I was going through my divorce. I could carry the weight of everything that was wrong in my life, or put the load down and wake up each day and decide to be happy, no matter what was going on. When we realise that happiness and unhappiness are choices, it frees us. It also prevents us from going into a negative spiral, where we will attract further bad karma." I saw a light bulb come on for Carla. "What you're saying is, that even though I feel disappointed, I can still choose to be happy each day?" A smile began to spread across Carla's face. "That's right. I'm not saying that you shouldn't feel and honour the feelings of sadness and disappointment over Oliver – of course you can do that. But then choose to move on to happiness."

Healing

The journey of healing never ends. Even when we have conquered one area of difficulty in our lives, along comes another challenge to face. It is wise to accept that life is a series of challenges and we have a choice to be open to them and to grow, or to be closed to them and become resentful and stagnant. Developing an active interior life within you is the key to facing challenges and healing. By making healing a priority in our lives, the healthier and happier we will be, the more able we will be to handle life's challenges and the more likely we will be to succeed in achieving what it is we want. If there are issues that have come up for you while reading this book which you feel unable to shift yourself, I would strongly recommend a healing therapy such as counselling, NLP, kinesiology or Reiki to shift old patterns. Sometimes an outside person who is totally objective can make the difference you need. However, healing ourselves is also a necessary investment, and can be done each and every day. Different forms of healing work for different people, and there is no right or wrong way. The following is a list of suggestions for self-healing.

Meditation is a highly effective healing form. Through meditation, we become more aware of living life in the present; not in thoughts about the past or thoughts about the future. When we do this, we choose "divine right action" in each and every moment. Many people believe they "can't meditate" because their minds are too busy, but that is precisely the reason why they should meditate! Meditation can feel uncomfortable at first because your mind will crowd with thoughts. It will feel anything but relaxing! However, if you take the time to commit 20 minutes each day to sitting with your eyes closed or looking at a candle, and focus on the sound and feel of your breathing, you will begin to notice the inner chatter of your mind and you will learn to allow the thoughts to float by, but they will no longer bother you. It is the accessing of this "observer" part of you that is transformational. You realise you are not the chattering mind, and that there is a higher part of your being, "the observer". When you get to know this part of yourself, life no longer feels as heavy. You realise you are "in it" but not "of it". To gain any benefit from meditation, it is important to commit to doing it every day.

Writing is cathartic. It helps relieve anxiety and other emotional states. Write for 10 to 15 minutes each day. Begin by writing what is on your mind, even if it is "I don't know what to write". Keep pen to paper without stopping, allowing a pure stream of consciousness to flow. Write down everything that is bothering you, literally "emptying" your mind. When you have finished writing, take a break, and then go back to what you have written. Notice any themes that may have come up. Then destroy what you have written. By doing this, you are enabling yourself to write candidly, knowing that it's all going to be destroyed afterwards.

Positive Affirmations assist in re-programming your thoughts and feelings. By saying how you wish to be or how you wish your life to be, you bring about more conscious awareness. Affirmations should be worded in "the now" in order to override past negative programming.

Yoga has powerful healing benefits. The more you open, stretch and strengthen your body, the more open, flexible and strong you will become in life. There are many types of yoga and if you are a beginner, I suggest you start with a teacher who will ensure you do the poses correctly.

Spending time in nature is a powerful healer. Walking, swimming, gardening, sailing or just sitting re-balances us. By being in nature, we become "at one" with it. I am always amazed at how my mood can alter after a long walk or a swim in the sea.

Painting, drawing or crafts are a wonderful way to heal if it is something you enjoy doing. When we practise an art form, we are creating, and therefore becoming one with the ultimate creator, The Universe.

Music is a powerful healer. Listen to music that raises your vibrations to that of inspiration, hope and joy.

Purpose

All of us need a sense of purpose and meaning in our lives. When we feel we are contributing to the world in our own unique way and making it a better place, we gain a deep sense of satisfaction. I hear many women tell me "I haven't found my purpose yet." Finding what one's purpose is can be a process and many don't discover it until later on in life. Some know what it is, but are unable to achieve it yet due to financial constraints or other blocks. Others are fortunate enough to be fulfilling their life purpose in their present career. Wherever you are with regards to your purpose, trust that you are exactly where you are meant to be right now. If you are unsure of what it is you are meant to be doing with your life, trust that the answer will come to you as your life unfolds. Focus on the role you do now, practise gratitude by being mindful of all the positives this job offers, and do it to the best of your ability. When we are fully present and focused in what we do and do it with love, even if it is a job not of our choosing, we cannot help but feel a sense of personal satisfaction. If you know what it is that you wish to do, but are unable to do it at present, make your wish your goal and visualise it on a regular basis. Take action by doing at least one thing towards that goal, no matter how small, such as reading a book on the subject, talking to someone who is in the field or signing up for a course. Don't give up on your dream, and enjoy the journey between now and when you attain it. Trust in the Universe to provide the opportunities that lead you to your goal.

Passion

Have you ever thought about what makes your heart sing? Do you have a special interest? Do you love doing a particular activity and when you do it, you lose all sense of time? This is being in the Universal Flow. Spending time doing something you love benefits you as a person on many levels:

- You increase your talent and ability.

- You increase your self-esteem.

- You feel more joyful.

- You open up the possibility of this becoming your life purpose, career and livelihood.

- You become a more interesting person.

The following subjects are based on the conversations I have most regularly with my single clients.

Dating

If you want an authentic long-term relationship and also wish to protect your heart along the way, it's important to see a first date as an introductory meeting, a platform upon which two people can get to know each other. Many women believe that, because they have been out on one or two dates with a man, they should invest themselves in this "new relationship". However, until you get to know anyone on a deeper level, it's unwise to invest too much of yourself in any one person. It's also unwise to give more than a man gives you in the early stages of dating. Investing too much can lead to disappointment and feelings of resentment. If we see dating as experimental and take it lightly, then it can be fun and relaxed. There is nothing wrong with dating more than one man at a time, as long as you have not committed or given the impression to someone that you are "exclusive" to him. Many women commit too early, without enough knowledge of their prospective mate. This makes it difficult and painful further down the track when they discover that their perceived perfect love is not who they thought they were and disappointed them.

In the early phases of a relationship, it is natural that we show only our most attractive qualities, however, usually after about three months, our flaws begin to appear. Thus it's wise to wait before committing and never to assume you are in an "exclusive relationship" until you feel sure that he's right for you, and that you have both agreed that you are. Remember too that as much as you want to reveal only your best qualities, being your authentic self from the beginning will ensure whether or not he likes you just the way you are.

"Booty calls" for pure sex are a high-risk choice, although some do turn into relationships. A man who isn't willing to go out with you in the more conventional way isn't giving you very much. I recommend to my clients that if they truly value themselves, they will wait for a man to ask them on a date.

Online Dating

Internet dating sites are prolific and many women are unsure whether to go online. I encourage any woman to trust her instincts on this. While I have heard many horror online dating stories, there are also happy couples that have met on dating sites. It is important that if you make the choice to date online, you keep open eyes, and realise that some people go online for different reasons than to find a life partner. Be sure to read profiles thoroughly to determine whether the person is in fact looking for a long-term relationship or not. Some women go online because they don't get to meet many men in their line of work or with their particular lifestyle. (In this case, it's a good idea to ensure you find outside interests, whether or not you use dating sites). What needs to be considered is the energy and intention underlying the choice to seek a partner on the Internet. If you are genuinely looking for your life partner and are willing to work on yourself, and to treat each first date as an "interview", you have a far greater chance of meeting someone online than someone who is "desperately" searching.

The downside of online dating is that a written profile and photograph cannot convey the energy of a person; it is only by meeting them that you can gauge this. Add to this the tendency for many to display photographs of themselves ten years younger, describe themselves as 10 centimetres taller and 10 kilograms lighter, and you could be in for a string of disappointments. Likewise, be totally honest in your own profile about yourself, your intentions, your interests and your photograph. If you meet someone and there is no chemistry it is better to say so, and do not suggest being friends as it is highly unlikely to work. If you are shy or easily put off, online dating is probably not for you. However, if you decide to take it lightly and see it as a fun journey, it can be a great opportunity to improve social dating skills.

Some friends and I signed up to an online dating site for a few months when we were single, and decided to treat it as a light-hearted adventure. While we all experienced our share of disappointments, we learned a lot about others and ourselves and enjoyed a good laugh along the way. It also helped me to see that there are many out there, both men and women, looking for love, and the world is full of possibilities.

The First Date

You can tell a lot about a man during the first date. In fact most of us, if we look back at past relationships, can probably remember first dates with ex-partners, and how the warning signs of their negative traits were already there. So many women don't ask enough questions in the initial getting-to-know-you period, and find themselves let down in the long-run by issues that would have raised alarm bells early on if only they had asked some important questions. Why don't women ask these essential questions? The main reason is that they want the fun of flirtation and romance only. Many of us don't want to know the negative traits of someone – we would prefer to stick our head in the sand and fill in the blanks with wishful thinking. Many of us see romance as an escape from reality (also called denial), and yet we pay a heavy price for it by becoming emotionally and sexually attached to a person who we're not going to be happy with in the long run. If your aim is to find your long-term partner, it is time to take a more grown up approach to dating. During the first date, you will want to get a realistic idea of who this man is. By asking some essential questions, you will be saving yourself time and heartache. Ask him questions based on your own values and what you are wanting. Here are some questions that may be helpful, and the possible warning bells you may receive. Be sure to ask when you are in a one-on-one conversation. If there is rarely an opportunity for one-on-one conversation, see that as a warning bell.

Where did he grow up? Does he have siblings? What are his parents like? (*Warning bell:* If he doesn't speak well of his family, he is bound to have emotional baggage).

Has he ever been married or lived with someone before? (*Warning bell:* If he is unwilling to talk about the past, he has a secretive nature, which is not a characteristic that bodes well for a long-term relationship. If he has had many short-term relationships or long-distance long-term relationships, he may be commitment phobic).

Why did it end? (*Warning bell:* If he blames his ex entirely for the failure of the relationship without acknowledging any fault of his own, he'll probably do the same in his next relationship).

What's his relationship like with his ex(es)? (*Warning bell:* If he speaks badly about his ex(es), he hasn't forgiven and is still carrying emotional baggage from past relationships that he will bring into your relationship).

What does he want in life? (*Warning bell:* If he doesn't want at least some of the things you value highly, the relationship is doomed).

Does he want to marry in the future? (*Warning bell:* If he says no and marriage is what you want, take him at his word and move on).

Would he like to have children? (*Warning bell:* If he says no and children are what you want, take him at his word and move on).

What are his interests? (*Warning bell:* If they are nothing like yours, move on).

We can tell a lot about a person by their behaviour and how they choose to treat us. Here are some behaviours and possible warning bells.

Is he on time? (*Warning bell:* unless there is a valid reason and an apology, being late says you are not a high priority).

How does he treat other people? (The restaurant staff, others standing in the cinema queue). (*Warning bell:* being impolite to other people reveals an unkind nature or lack of empathy).

Does he look at other women? (*Warning bell:* Looking at other women while in your company reveals that he doesn't think you are worth giving all his attention to).

Does he send phone texts while in your company? (*Warning bell:* If he is in contact with other people while on a first date, he is unlikely to give you his full attention in the future).

Does he offer to pay for the date? (*Warning bell:* Offering to pay on a first date is a courteous and polite thing to do, even if you insist on going Dutch. If he doesn't offer, he either has financial problems or he is mean. Meanness usually extends to other areas of life too – love, time and things).

Does he ask you questions about yourself?
(*Warning bell:* If he doesn't ask anything about you, he's either not very interested in you or he is self-centred).

Is he willing to answer your questions? (*Warning bell:* If he's not willing to answer your questions, it reveals he is secretive, has something to hide and doesn't want you to know him).

How you feel when you are on a date is also a good barometer of whether the two of you have potential.

Do you feel comfortable? (*Warning bell:* While feeling a little nervous on a first date is normal, feelings of discomfort as the date continues signal that on a subconscious level, you have picked up on something that bothers you).

Do you want to know all about him? (*Warning bell:* If you do not want to get to know him, why are you going out with him? You're either using him for company or just not interested in him).

Do you feel attracted to him? (*Warning bell:* If there is no feeling of attraction by the end of a first date, it is unlikely that the attraction will grow).

Are you enjoying yourself? (*Warning bell:* If there is little enjoyment on a first date, it is unlikely there will be further enjoyment later on).

Finding out as much as you can about him in the early days of dating and being clear that he is the right person for you can be like building the foundations of a house. If the foundations are faulty, the house will have structural problems and will require constant fixing, and may even have to be demolished. It's best to start out with the right foundations in the first place.

Socialising

"Where can I go to meet men?" asked Simone. I have heard this question many times. "Go out because you want to go out, because you want to enjoy the company of your friends, because you want to do an activity you love, or even to flirt. But as soon as you decide you're going out in the hope of meeting someone, you're going to be disappointed," I replied. Simone looked perplexed. "But I *need* to be out in order to meet someone!" I explained to her my philosophy. When we go out "searching", either no one seems interested or we attract desperate men. Why is this? Because we are giving off desperate, predatory energy, which is a turn off to most men, except the desperate ones who are matching our vibrational energy!

Masculine and Feminine Energy

I see many successful career women who are attractive, intelligent and successful, but find relationships difficult. Because women now have equal rights to men and are taking on roles that were traditionally male, they have taken on some of the masculine energy that is necessary to survive in the modern business world, but that is where it needs to remain. Male energy is proactive, assertive and goal oriented. Think of the archetype of the hunter. Men are hard-wired to chase. As old fashioned as it sounds, this is a fact and isn't likely to change. You can, however, put this knowledge to good use and make it work for you, by using your feminine energy. Female energy is receptive, creative and yielding. If a man is interested in you, allow him to lead the situation. In the early dating stage, ringing you and asking you out is his domain, not yours. Men enjoy a chase. If you're calling him and asking him out, you are using masculine energy, which can make a man want to run. If a woman becomes pushy, it robs the man of his desire to chase, and he will likely lose interest. If you feel that if you do not do something, nothing will ever happen, you may be right, but if a man isn't willing to make the first move, he is just not interested enough. You are not going to make things better by being pro-active. While this may frustrate you, see it as a gift that can give you clarity easily. It can relieve you of a lot of unnecessary angst, because if a man is interested in you enough, he will make it clear and do something about it.

There is possibly one exception to this, and that is when a man is extremely shy or lacks confidence, in which case go ahead and ask him out on a first date. At the end of the date, if you have had an enjoyable time, let him know it, tell him you would love to see him again and that you will wait to hear from him. Afterwards, allow him the space to make the next move.

Sex

A strange thing happens to a woman when she sleeps with a man. She feels bonded to him, even if he is the wrong person for her. And while a man may enjoy it immensely, these feelings are not necessarily reciprocated as men are wired differently. This inevitably leads to an undesirable outcome – a woman falling head over heels for potentially the wrong man and wasting time in a relationship that is not going to work in the long run, not to mention the ensuing heartbreak and disappointment. Most of us have made the mistake of going to bed with a man too soon, for various reasons.

- "We'd been out twice"

- "I hadn't been with someone in ages and I couldn't resist"

- "He took me out for dinner and it felt so romantic"

- "I've been lonely"

- "I felt it was expected"

- "The sexual attraction was just too strong".

We are all human and a need for physical connection and touch is normal. However, if you want to find someone to be with in the long term, it is wise to hold off as long as you can. If you are in the habit of going to bed with a man in the very early days of a new relationship, here are some questions to ask yourself:

- Do I love myself enough to believe that my company is gratuity enough?

- Do I respect myself enough to endure another night alone in my own bed, above future heartbreak?

- Do I like him enough to get to know him more before we become lovers?

- Am I willing to have the foresight to see what I am creating by falling into bed with someone too soon?

I'd be the first to say that the above questions are pretty boring, however many women see a date as a "romantic escape", in which they lose their heads. It may feel wonderful at the time, but there is no thought as to future consequences. Most of us have felt the pain of heartbreak and rejection and know how it can affect us deeply on all levels. If you want to keep such feelings to a minimum, delayed gratification is a wise choice. A man who likes and respects you will be willing to wait for a sexual union. While sexual chemistry can be overwhelming, it doesn't necessarily lead to a happy long-term union. Many people incorrectly think that because there is a huge sexual attraction, they are "meant to be together". Sadly, many of these relationships turn out to be quite combustible, unless there are also other elements that unite the couple. The aim here is to hold off on sex as long as possible, in order to see how you connect on all the other levels first. I have certainly learned this through my own personal experience.

The Biological Clock

Many of my clients are women who are in their 30's who are worried that their time is running out to become a mother. If you fear not meeting someone in time to have child, acknowledge the fear. What would your life be like if you didn't have children? I hear many women say "I can't bear to think what my life would be like if I can't have children." They see their lives as following one possible trajectory only, and any other possibility is unthinkable and seen as a catastrophe. However, while the arrival of children can bring wonder, joy, love and growth into our lives; it also brings responsibility, loss of freedom, huge sacrifice and stress. It is important to acknowledge the "positives" of not having children.

Women who want children but are unable to have them experience feelings of desperation and an overwhelming sense of missing out, but they are also able to pursue their life purpose/career without feeling emotionally drained or guilty, to experience relationships without the stress that children can bring and to grow in ways that women who have children cannot. It's important to face one's "worst possible scenario", as it is a reality for some women, and to put faith in the Universe that if you are meant to have them, the right partner will come along in time. If you are not meant to have them, a different path awaits you and it can be a wonderful path. Fear, as we know, attracts what we don't want. If you can surrender to this way of thinking, you will release the feelings of fear and desperation around finding a mate in time, and change your energy into that of allowing.

Mary, a deputy principle in a primary school in her 40's, told me of the moment she looked out of her office window and saw the mothers kissing goodbye their little ones on their first day of school, and how she cried with the realisation that she probably would never have children. However, something else also happened as she let go of that dream; she opened up to another dream. She applied for a position overseas and has lived in Hong Kong for the past eight years. Her life is full – an interesting career, travel to exotic places and amazing personal growth.

If you want to beat the biological clock, meeting someone who you are compatible with and is also ready to start a family is the key. Some women stay in a relationship on the assumption that at some point their partner will be ready for children, even though they have never had this confirmed verbally. I have seen women who have felt they have wasted years of their lives with a man they assumed they would marry and have children to, only to be told some years into the relationship that he never wanted that. Never assume anything! If you are over 35 and wanting children, the conversation needs to happen within six months of meeting this person, and even if you are younger, don't leave the conversation too long. If you meet someone you like, ask him the important questions early on, and whether he wants to have children. Focus on getting to know him before you go to bed with him. If you feel that this relationship has potential, be mindful of whether it's progressing. Has it been established that the two of you are dating exclusively? If there has been no conversation about where the two of you are headed, initiated by him, within three months, then it is only right that you instigate the conversation and listen carefully to his reply. Here are some possible answers to the question "Are we exclusive?" and how to respond.

- "I'm not ready for an exclusive relationship" – take his answer at face value and move on. He's not ready for a relationship!

- "I'm not sure" - move on. He's not ready for a relationship!

- "I really like you but I feel like you're pressuring me" – move on. He's not ready for a relationship!

- "Yes. I'd like to be" – continue the relationship and see where it goes.

- "I assumed we were already exclusive" – continue the relationship and see where it goes.

If the relationship does progress, you will need to convey at some point over the next few months your desire for children and that you don't want to leave it too late. This should have been conveyed during the very early stages of dating, so should come as no surprise. How does he feel about that? Again, listen to the answer. Here are some possible replies and how it would be best to respond.

- "I don't think I want children" – move on. He doesn't want children!

- "I'm not ready to have children" – ask him when he might be. If he's unsure, not willing to be clear or gives you a time a long way in the future, move on. He won't be having children with you.

- "I feel like you're pressuring me" – explain to him the issue of your body clock. If he is empathic to your situation and willing to talk about it and be open to the idea of children, you will need to choose whether or not to stay in the relationship based on how long you are willing to wait.

- "Yes, but not now" – ask him "When?" If he gives a time frame that is acceptable, continue the relationship and follow up on the subject when the proposed time comes. If he is unsure, you must choose whether or not to stay in the relationship based on how long you are willing to wait.

- "Yes" – continue the relationship and make plans.

If a man loves you and wants children, he will be willing to have children with you. If you are over 35, have been in a relationship for a year and he feels it's too soon to have a child, you need to ask him the question "Do you love me enough to give me what I want, at the expense of some inconvenience to yourself?"

Dating when you have children

Jane was divorced and had two children, 12 and 9, who lived mostly with her. She was ready for a relationship. She decided to go on an Internet dating site, and after a few months she met Paul and they began going out every Saturday night. Paul was also divorced with children, although he only took care of them every second weekend. After a month, he suggested to Jane that they get together with the children for a barbeque on the Saturday night he looked after his children. Jane felt uncomfortable about this, but was also flattered that he wanted the families to meet so quickly. She thought that this must mean that he was serious about her. The evening went well and the children got along. Soon they were in the habit of "joining families" whenever Paul had his children until, three months into their relationship, Paul's attention began to cool off. He called her less often and didn't seem as happy and as present as he had been to begin with. Jane wondered what was going on, and followed a gut instinct. She went to her computer and pulled up the dating site where she had met Paul. His profile was still on the site, and she could see his "activity history". His last interaction had been the night before. Jane was devastated and confronted Paul, who told her that they had never agreed that they were "exclusive". Jane was left to deal with not only her own heartache, but also her children's. Whether you decide to go online or meet people through other means, keep your dating life private from your children. Children don't thrive in an environment where Mum has a succession of boyfriends. Just as it is important to protect your own heart and emotions, it's important to protect your children's. Introduce your children to a new partner only when you have both verbally agreed you are in a committed exclusive relationship. Be sure that you decide when the children will meet him; it is not up to your partner.

Commitment

I have heard clients say, "He's not committed enough". My response to them is "He's either committed or he isn't". Commitment doesn't necessarily come in the form of a wedding ring. Commitment shows itself by his being there for you during difficult times as well as happy times, his treating you as a high priority, his sexual and emotional fidelity and a willingness to make it known that you are a couple. I have counselled married women who are in relationships that are clearly not committed – they are more like living arrangements. On the other hand, I know unmarried women who are in deeply satisfying, committed relationships.

Trust Your Own Instincts

Too many women obsess over what a man does and how he is behaving, as opposed to observing their own behaviours and reactions. Learn to trust yourself and your instincts. Trust in your body and its sensations – it is rarely wrong. Here are some signs that he's probably not for you.

- If you're already thinking he needs counselling

- If you're reading books or internet sites trying to work him out

- If you're thinking he has potential, and you're working out ways you could "fix him"

- If you're visiting psychics to find the answers

- If you feel emotionally upset on a regular basis

Finding Someone Who Treats You Well

We teach others how we want to be treated by how we treat ourselves and others, and showing them our expectations. If a man calls you at the last minute to ask you out, don't say yes unless it really is convenient for you also. You are teaching him that you are not someone to ask out at his convenience. If he doesn't like that and doesn't ask you out again, take that as confirmation that he did see you as a convenience! Be true to yourself first and don't cancel your personal plans for him. If there are things he does that upset or irritate you early on, tell him. If he refuses to acknowledge how you feel about it or make an effort to improve things, be strong enough to walk away. If he's not willing to make some adjustments in the early stages, he'll be unlikely to want to make any changes later on.

Trust

The only person who can protect your heart and soul is you. It's unwise to trust anybody too early. The right man will appreciate a woman who takes responsibility for her own life and respects herself. Trust must be earned and not just instantly expected, and we must learn to trust ourselves before we can trust anyone else. This means trusting your own inner guidance and using all of your senses to know if someone is worthy of your trust. It is normal to have trust issues with a new partner if you were betrayed in a previous relationship. If this is what is happening for you, remain aware that you may be overly suspicious because of a previous betrayal, but stay open also to the idea that it may be your intuition telling you that something isn't right. Allow your fear of further betrayal AND your basic intuition to work for you. My client Lee's new partner told her she had a trust issue because of her previous partner's affair, but rather than being understanding and wanting her to feel secure, he seemed to go out of his way to ensure she felt suspicious and insecure. Lee may have had a trust issue based on a past relationship trauma, but her intuition was telling her that this man was not the right person for her either. In a healthy relationship, both partners want the other to feel emotionally safe. If you have a pattern of sabotaging relationships because you feel unable to trust, seeking counselling, NLP or kinesiology would be of benefit.

When You Realise He's Not for You

There is no "painless" way of ending a relationship that isn't working for you if the other person really likes you. There is, however, a way in which you will inflict the least pain in the long term, and that is to end it as soon as possible. Be direct and once you have made the decision, stick to it. Be as honest as you can as to why you don't wish to take things further, but keep it impersonal as well. For example, if you aren't attracted to him enough, say you just don't feel any chemistry between you. This takes the focus off him and onto the "intangible". If you don't like his lifestyle or his friends, tell him you don't think you have enough in common. There is no point in going into detail if you feel it isn't right. If he insists on trying to convince you otherwise, stay firm and tell him you have already made up your mind. Suggesting to remain friends may be a ploy to stay in touch in the hope of things developing. This will not be a comfortable nor equal friendship. Don't agree to be friends just because you feel guilty or feel sorry for him. This is not a good basis for a friendship. Once you have ended it, cut contact. It may seem drastic and cruel, but it is the best and kindest way for both of you to heal and move on quickly.

When He Tells You You're Not for Him

Let's face it. Rejection hurts. Just as most of us dislike hurting someone else, we also dislike being hurt. There is nothing pleasant about it, but looking at it from a "bigger picture" perspective can help. In order to find the right person, we are bound to meet a number of others first, and they all come along to teach us something. When we get hurt in love, we can choose to take it personally and feel defective, angry and bitter or we can see it as a lesson in love that we were meant to have. "Just how many lessons do I need?". As many as you are meant to have. Lessons keep coming even after we have found love.

IN CONCLUSION

FINDING LOVE IS A PROCESS

It is a spiritual journey all of its own

We are meant to dance the dance of finding a mate. The choice is ours as to whether or not we enjoy it. It will entail some highs and some lows, and learning a lot about others and ourselves as we go. We may have our hearts broken and learn some hard lessons, but they are all for our highest good and growth. With each lesson learned, the more we are able to listen to that still, small voice inside us which will guide us in the right direction. And when we choose to learn the lessons, we become greater, and adjust our ideas of who it is we are and whom it is we want to be with.

When you find him, the journey doesn't end. There will be a new journey with new challenges. There will be highs and lows, fulfilment and disappointment, happiness and sorrow. After all, how are we to ever appreciate the Light unless we have walked awhile in the dark?

ACTION PLAN

5 STEPS TO FINDING LOVE

1. Have a love affair with yourself

    a. Practise affirmations on self-love to override old incorrect beliefs

    b. Look in the mirror each day and say "I love you"

    c. Practise healthy routines with food and exercise

    d. Practise gratitude for what you have right now

    e. Spend some time alone if you feel lonely and allow the feeling to be there

    f. Get help for addictions

    g. Treat yourself as you would like to be treated by a lover or a best friend

    h. Join a club or take up a new interest if your life feels empty

  i. Practise gratitude for all the qualities you like in yourself.

2. Change Your Beliefs

  a. Practise positive affirmations on men and relationships to override old beliefs that no longer serve you

  b. Excavate any other negative beliefs that no longer serve you and create and practise new positive affirmations to override them

  c. Excavate your reasons for wanting a relationship and create and practise new positive affirmations to override any reasons that do not serve you

  d. Become aware of negative thoughts by being aware of how you feel in your body

  e. Practise reframing negative thoughts to positive ones

  f. Be patient and believe in Divine Universal Timing

3. Change Your Patterns

a. Excavate any patterns in your choice of men to date that have not served you

b. Excavate any patterns within yourself to date that have not served you

c. Own your negative patterns and stay aware of them so as not to repeat them

d. If negative patterns prove difficult to break, seek outside help

e. Take things slowly in new relationships and become "the observer"

f. View previous negative relationship experiences as necessary lessons you had to have to make you a better person

g. Stop rescuing, or being rescued!

h. If a rescuing pattern is difficult to shift, seek outside help

i. Keep heart and head balanced when choosing a partner

j. Stay aware of the 9 types of men to avoid

k. Forgive all those who have hurt you

l. Forgive yourself.

4. Clarify What It Is You Want

    a. Establish your list of values

    b. Become clear of what kind of relationship it is you want

    c. Create a wish list for the qualities you would like in a partner

    d. Visualise and imagine the relationship you desire until you feel happy

    e. Detach from the outcome

    f. Practise gratitude for what you have now

    g. Create a vision board

    h. Create reminders and signs for display to remind you not to give up.

5. Make Wise Choices In the Present

    a. Choose happiness – it's a choice

    b. Practise self-healing – meditation, writing, positive affirmations, yoga, time in nature, art and crafts, music

    c. Be on purpose

    d. Follow your passions and interests

e. Date as many men as you want – just be honest about it

f. Find out as much as you can about a man on the first date and ask him the important questions early on

g. Use your feminine energy; avoid using masculine energy

h. Postpone sex in a new relationship for as long as you can

i. If your biological clock is ticking, establish whether he wants children early on and do not stay too long in a relationship with a man who doesn't want children if that is what you want

j. If you have children, do not involve them in your dating life until you are in an exclusive, committed relationship

k. Learn to trust your intuition more

l. Teach others how to treat you by valuing and treating yourself well.

m. Do not trust others blindly; trust must be earned.

GLOSSARY OF HEALING ARTS SUGGESTED IN THIS BOOK

The following are healing techniques which I have suggested throughout this book, should the reader feel they need to do further healing.

Counselling/Psychotherapy – talking therapy. The difference between these two techniques can best be described as this. While counselling is snorkelling, psychotherapy is scuba diving. Counselling is used to resolve issues on a more superficial level; psychotherapy goes deeper in order to resolve deep emotional issues. There are many different techniques that counsellors and psychotherapists use to enable a person to become more self-aware and instigate change. Counselling is a process, and may require 3-4 sessions; psychotherapy will probably require a longer commitment, in order to gain rewarding results. Both therapists will assist you in processing old issues that haven't been resolved, bring about awareness to core beliefs and patterns and help instigate the behavioural changes needed.

Psychodrama – used by counsellors and psychotherapists, this technique uses deep action methods and re-enactment of events to explore and correct issues. By being in a "total body" experience, the client is able to "de-intellectualise" an issue and access every part of herself.

Kinesiology – Kinesiology encompasses holistic health disciplines which use the gentle art of muscle monitoring to access information about a person's wellbeing. It combines Western techniques and Eastern wisdom to promote physical, emotional, mental and spiritual health. Kinesiology identifies the elements which inhibit the body's natural internal energies and accesses the life enhancing potential within the individual.

NLP – Neuro Linguistic Programming is a transformative process that brings awareness around how we think and communicate, allowing behavioural and emotional change. NLP can free up a person's thinking process, allowing them to see many other possibilities and to have a better understanding of their motivations and behaviours. NLP can bring about immediate positive change to negative behaviours and emotional states.

Reiki – Reiki is an ancient Japanese energetic healing therapy that boosts and balances the life force energy, "Ki". Not only does it heal on all levels – physical, emotional, mental and spiritual – it can assist in clearing past issues as it heals on a cellular level. Everything that has ever happened to us is held in our cells. Reiki is a relaxing, non-invasive therapy and a course of at least four sessions is necessary to make lasting changes.

ABOUT THE AUTHOR

Nicole Bayliss is a Holistic Counsellor, Reiki Master and NLP Practitioner. She lectures and holds workshops in Meditation and Creating the Life You Want. Nicole is passionate about assisting others to reach their full potential in all areas of their lives. She lives and practises in Mosman, Sydney.

www.ingramcontent.com/pod-product-compliance
Lightning Source LLC
Chambersburg PA
CBHW021404090426
42742CB00009B/999